A NEW
DYNAMIC
EFFECTIVE
BUSINESS IN
A CIRCULAR
ECONOMY

Edited by
Ken Webster, Jocelyn Blériot
and Craig Johnson
Ellen MacArthur Foundation

Ellen MacArthur Foundation
The Sail Loft
42 Medina Road
Cowes
Isle of Wight
PO31 7BX
United Kingdom

www.ellenmacarthurfoundation.org

Designed by Graham Pritchard.
Copy editing by Samantha Guerrini.
Printed by Seacourt using 100% renewable
energy-the world's first zero waste printer.

Printed on revive 100 Offset a recycled grade
containing 100% post consumer waste and
manufactured at a mill accredited with ISO14001
environmental management standard.
The pulp used in this product is bleached
using a Totally Chlorine Free process (TCF).

FOREWORD

The idea of the circular economy is capturing the attention of businesses, academics and the next generation of entrepreneurs as a framework for re-designing the economy. Over the past three years since the inception of the Foundation, we have seen it inspire new thinking as an alternative economic model which can be both restorative and regenerative, working to create effective material and energy flows. It is distinctly different from our current linear take, make, dispose economy and is as relevant to developing countries as to developed markets.

The circular economy however is a synthesis of ideas led by pioneers such as William McDonough and Michael Braungart with 'cradle to cradle'; Amory B Lovins and natural capitalism; Janine Benyus and biomimicry; Walter Stahel and the performance/sharing economy and including insights from industrial ecology. Inspired by this model the Foundation has not only the goal of building insight, but also to work with businesses and educators from across the world to turn analysis into reality, thus, accelerating the transition to a circular economy. This book has brought together many of these leading thinkers and practitioners and provides their insights into product and system design, business models, construction and urban design and the application of systems thinking to energy and materials flows. The aim is to stimulate, engage and highlight new opportunities for entrepreneurs and established businesses.

To create further momentum around the model we have worked to produce economic reports with analysis by McKinsey & Co. that have highlighted benefits in excess of USD 1 trillion. Wider engagement includes the Foundation's CE100 business platform, work with the World Economic Forum and more in depth work with our Global Partners Philips, Cisco, Renault, Kingfisher and Unilever. In addition to our work with business the Foundation works with many of the world's leading universities* through our global Schmidt MacArthur Fellowship and Pioneer Universities Programmes to further develop our understanding of the circular economy through research and teaching.

As a global systems level change it involves so much opportunity, and it is the aim of this book to help to further understanding and engagement in its realisation.

Ellen MacArthur

*UC Berkeley, Cranfield University, Imperial College London, Kedge Business School, London Business School, MIT Massachusetts Institute of Technology, MIP Politecnico Di Milano, National Institute of Design, India, Stanford University, Tongji University, TU Delft, Yale University and University of Bradford

"THE THEORY DETERMINES WHAT WE OBSERVE"

Albert Einstein

THE DECLINE OF THE LINEAR ECONOMY AND THE RISE OF THE CIRCULAR
A STORY ABOUT FRAMEWORKS AND SYSTEMS

1

Ken Webster

The linear economy emerged and sprang from an era of exploration and scientific revolution. Driven by money as debt into rapid and escalating growth, it worked well so long as there were plentiful resources, especially energy. However, a new way of seeing the world based on our times is emerging. The circular economy entrains systems in a virtuous cycle of capital building. Much has changed which makes this decade the gateway to the circular economy.

Ken Webster is Head of Innovation, Ellen MacArthur Foundation. He is a major contributor to the development of ideas around the circular economy. As Honorary Teaching Fellow at Bradford University School of Management he teaches on the Innovation, Enterprise and Circular Economy MBA.

ken.webster@ellenmacarthurfoundation.org

Ellen MacArthur Foundation
www.ellenmacarthurfoundation.org

Important ideas seem to take some time to emerge fully into the daylight. Perhaps this is because ideas do not exist in an intellectual vacuum, and they have consequences. There are winners and losers and reputations to be maintained – or lost – as well the impact of any application of an idea in the world of materials and energy. Max Planck thought that ideas would succeed when the supporters of the old retired and died, i.e. change can occur with the change of generations. That may be part of it but once underway change is profound and has no respect for age or reputation. Victor Hugo noted: "An invasion of armies can be resisted but not an idea whose time has come." How much more is this the case when it is not merely an idea but the framework of understanding which underpins an age, the root metaphors of our thinking of how the world works which is in play.

For such a change in prospect, before our day, we have to go back to the 17th century. In Newton's time, the idea of a clockwork universe took about 70 years to be accepted. This seems surprising to the modern age as it is surely common sense to see the world as 'machine like'. More than that, it seems commonplace to seek out the 'scientifically proven' and the rational. The world as machine or mechanism 'framing' tells us that the world is, in principle understandable, predictable, controllable... Isn't it all a done deal? Well, no, not then it wasn't. Perhaps not now, either, but for a different reason.

For most of human history the way of the world was as much or more about the divine or demonic, the spirit and fate, obligation or chance. Business was far from free, controlled as it was by guilds, licensed as monopolies by popes, kings and queens and weighed down with tradition. The world as machine was such a fine idea however, as it was used to search for the building blocks and then the mechanisms in every one of the emerging disciplines: in physics, chemistry, medicine, engineering, biology, (where Darwin had such an influence at a later date). It had application and was just a better way of getting things done, it had consequence and the industrial revolution was just one. The idea applied as much in the social realm through the new studies of psychology, sociology and of course in that branch of natural philosophy called economics, all of which soon wanted to be quantitative sciences. In economics the market became the mechanism for deciding resource allocation, and the individual as consumer and as business (producer) or worker was best served by a free exchange, open information, many buyers and sellers and the rational, welfare maximising 'homo economicus'[1]. Anything less would restrict the market mechanism.

More broadly, the individual as the 'atom of society' was not only able to make his or her own approach to the Divine, rather than through the priest: to be able to read the Bible in her own language, but she was also to begin the shaking off of irrational arrangements in all else, from social duties to business, to denounce them as in the example above, a hindrance on trade – the rationale of trade being the market. It became commonplace to point to the individual, or the individual business (when they became legal entities as corporations) as the rational focus for all economic choices and benefits deployed through the market. Welcome to the modern world. And it worked. For a time it was almost deified as 'Progress' with a capital 'P'. This ended in its naïve sense in the 1950s and 1960s, when such grand metanarratives were dismissed by a more cynical populace and the post modern theorists[2].

An end point for a society encouraged by marketeers and popular culture to think of 'me and mine' is, ironically, to reject the ideologies they see around them. But it is worth tracing this line even so, since it held sway for several hundred years and its prints are everywhere and economics still seems most resistant to change.

The modern world became the expression of an idea or framework, and in common with all abstract ideas – these grand metanarratives – it used a self referencing set of metaphors to express its meaning. This is the 'world as machine' metaphor, unsurprisingly. Everywhere we look in this era there are 'mechanisms', which are 'regulated', or 'driven', or 'built in.' Remember the Iron Law of Wages, Say's Law, Darwinian 'survival of the fittest'?

Some mechanisms are built to transmit power – real or social – or transmit plain old information. In schools those that know are assumed to teach those that do not, by 'transmitting' knowledge or drills and skills upon which the proto worker-machines are tested and then graded. Education proper is reserved for those who are to be in charge, their horizons remaining unbounded as befits those who are more likely to design the machines for producing wealth or whose families control the stock (shareholdings).

Bureaucracies transmit instructions and discipline themselves according to standard operating procedures. Modernism is the age of Fordism, of dreadful experiments with mass social engineering through fascism and communism. All of it is dressed up under the aegis of the world as machine and the notion, therefore, that society is perfectable in the way that a locomotive might be with the right parts in the right order.

The mechanisms throughout are deemed (as they must be – just consider the word 'mechanism') impersonal, lifeless and inexorable, unforgiving just like the machine, but being rational, oh so beautiful for all that. Some of these notions were and still are reflected in preferences for straight lines, machined surfaces; in the geometrics and order of buildings and towns built to right angle grids, counting off roads, avenue addresses by number, or designing 'machines to live in' (Le Corbusier), the increasing dismissal of ornament and above all – driving it, in fact – the search for the efficient. Thus, so often is largeness and scale celebrated, because this is meant to be efficiency deployed in a grand manner. It was an era of mass production and mass consumption. And in resource and energy terms the economy was a machine for turning materials and energy into producer and consumer goods and services and, since resources and resourcefulness were as endless as the oil gushing from the wells of West Texas and Persia, more and faster and more efficiently was the key to surplus which in turn made everyone richer. A machine world, manufacturing prosperity endlessly, and thus prosperity in turn lifting like a rising tide all the boats which float upon it. Or, to pervert George Carlin the social commentator, 'you didn't have to be asleep to believe in the American dream'[3]. The blacktop led on forever and was best travelled in a V8 Dodge Challenger. More, faster and for me.

Thus the world of business is as embedded in the global spillover from the whole Enlightenment project as is western culture generally. Business is being affected by a number of profound changes surfacing in the 21st century, some of them economic, some recent, but many of them crises within society itself as it finds the dreams and expectations of past generations to be only loosely anchored in any form of reality[4].

All systems have histories and all systems tend to entrain, to draw in and shape relationships and material within their orbit. The linear throughput economy of translating materials into manufactures, or soils into food or fisheries into fish fingers via cheap energy, works with the following entrainment. A big industrial scale obtains efficiencies and thus cost advantages and usually competitive advantages. Big scale, big throughput means lots of consumption, not as a one off, but continuously. In the beginning, when skilled labour was scarce, it made sense to increase labour productivity. At that stage, since material and energy prices were falling on a long-term trend and technology was ever more effective, labour productivity could grow while still generating enough spending power for employees to purchase most of the products being made and paying enough taxes to clean up some of the externalised costs, as well as interest on loans and pension contributions. Prosperity spawned new industries and new employment opportunities. Externalities are a function of throughput. The responsibility transfers to the purchaser at point of sale and onward to the local authority and its taxpayers when it becomes waste. Linear systems at scale need demand to stay high, so disposal and planned, or other, obsolescences are welcome, perhaps even necessary. Novelty is a big plus, diversification and selling brand and lifestyle all help. Dividing up markets, differentiating and marketing effectively to the various niches follows. Just keep the flow going.

To create new markets, what was once free must be made scarce: the consumer is encouraged to look for convenience, to buy what he or she wants rather than rely on self, family or social capital. The ideal consumer is very dependent on marketed goods and services, so quite passive, if increasingly discerning.

The simple idea of mass production and consumption has long faded and something more complex has arisen. The consumer, increasingly likely to live alone or act autonomously, is sold lifestyle and meaning through products and services. The act of shopping is as much a part of the satisfaction as the product or service, especially in many European markets which are at saturation level, and replacement or substitution is all that remains. Consumers who don't actually need to buy 'stuff' can be persuaded by the experience, it seems. The role of brand, celebrity association and expectations is obvious. Choice has multiplied creating, paradoxically, more uncertainty and frustration just as other certainties erode around consumers: the idea of long-term employment, of house ownership, welfare benefits, pensions and insurance or endowment policies – and even employment contracts – which deliver on the original contract. Add in, post 2007/08, the squeeze on middle incomes, on credit, on the public service ('austerity' as part of the cost of bailing out the banks) and other forms of social contract, including the idea that savings should bring a modest return or that old age can be funded and care and dignity ensured.

Still, there is a vague sense of rising expectations but certainly it is more one of declining hope. The rising tide which was supposed to float all boats has failed to rise in this season, or if it does rise there seems to be a large marina now cut off from the sea in which it is possible to become stranded in the shallows, shuttling between low wages and unemployment[5]. Politicians can only suggest more economic growth but are at a loss to know from whence it will come.

It is easier to know where growth went. First, a look at the graph for commodities prices over the last 100 years (Figure 1) shows a remarkable turn around, from a fall of around 1.2% per annum on average to a post 2001 surge which has removed all the gains. Why would a business want to lose the materials that pass through its hands as a manufacturer or retailer when it will cost more, and create a degree of uncertainty around price and supply, to replace them year-on-year. What was once a clearway, a one-way street, has become risky, potholed and at times blocked – as consumers can do little to borrow and spend more.

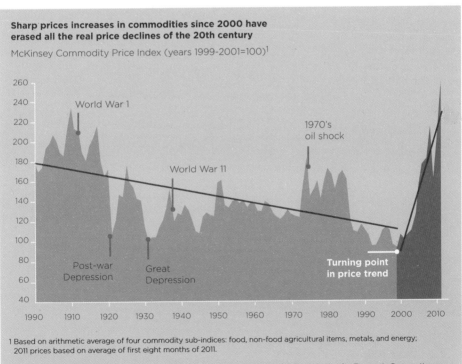

Sharp prices increases in commodities since 2000 have erased all the real price declines of the 20th century

McKinsey Commodity Price Index (years 1999-2001=100)[1]

1 Based on arithmetic average of four commodity sub-indices: food, non-food agricultural items, metals, and energy; 2011 prices based on average of first eight months of 2011.

Source: Grilli and Yang; Pfaffenzeller; World Bank; International Monetary Fund; Organisation for Economic Cooperation and Development statistics; UN Food and Agriculture Organization; UN Comtrade; Ellen MacArthur Foundation circular economy team

Figure 1 **Commodity prices 1900-2010**

Adding to this is the coming resource shocks from China and India and no doubt Russia, Brazil and South Africa (the so called BRICS) so that the upward trend looks to be continuous, if volatile (speculators are at work in these and all 'tight' markets and the Great Recession does not help). McKinsey & Company[6] characterised this shock by drawing out the doubling times for GDP for various nations and their populations. When it is realised that a country as populous as China is doubling its economy nearly every ten years then a certain troublesome feeling around materials and resources will be evident. It is not just the material costs which are at stake. In both this and the energy markets the question of security of supply looms large. Already, China, with almost all of the production of rare earth metals in its control – vital to the electronics and renewables industries – has cut supply on more than one occasion in defiance of WTO rules.

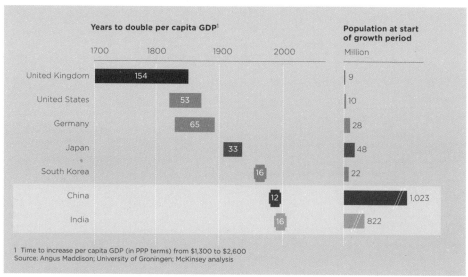

1 Time to increase per capita GDP (in PPP terms) from $1,300 to $2,600
Source: Angus Maddison; University of Groningen; McKinsey analysis

Figure 2 **Incomes are rising in developing economies faster - and on a greater scale - than at any previous point in history**

Secondly, this dyspepsia is aggravated by a look at energy production figures over the recent decade. A kind of plateau has been reached with easy and accessible oil supply (so called conventional oil) very much failing to respond to price – remembering that at the beginning of the period (2000) oil was around USD 10 a barrel and, even on the edge of another recession, Brent Crude now stays stickily around USD 100. Lack of responsiveness to price usually means real supply constraints and a look at where new oil is coming from confirms the challenge: from miles under the seabed in an operation which rivals landing men on the moon in complexity; from sticky tar sand; from barely-oil-at-all shale formations. In economic terms, oil at around USD 150 a barrel seems to be all an economy can take before tumbling back into recession[7]. It is not the amount of oil in the ground that matters but its rate of supply, its financial and, of course, its energy cost, the so-called EROEI (energy return on energy invested). The original discoveries in Saudi Arabia had an energy cost of around one barrel of oil to deliver 100 barrels to the refinery, while nowadays the tar sands ratio is more like 1:5 or less.

At this stage there needs to be a confession of sorts. This picture is painted with two assumptions. Firstly, that real resource limits matter in economics (especially energy, but also materials including food). Even if a disruptive technology or markets might change resource relationships it both takes a time to get under way and requires investment. In short it requires a surplus to be available for creating any new infrastructure. The world has known for more than 40 years that this situation would be pressing and it has done little or nothing about it[8].

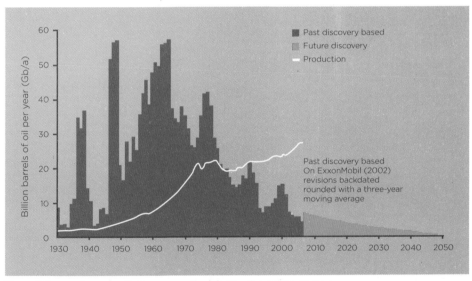

Figure 3 **The growing gap: oil, discovery and production (conventional oil)**

The other assumption is that money is not neutral, that banks and financial institutions are not just intermediaries, putting money to work which would otherwise be idle. Money created as debt in advance of production (credit) is almost alchemical, turning crude ideas and raw materials and energy into profits, wages and welfare from nothing[9]. Behind all resources and energy discussion there is another driver, one which is little known in this context, but one which entrains the productive economy from the start. It is money issued as debt. In the modern era almost all money is issued as debt when banks make loans (approximately 97%). The interest on the money is not created, just the principal, and this interest money must be found somewhere. The economic actors must be more competitive to secure enough to repay loans. Increasing productivity and cheap oil have combined and reinforced each other to increase output and that surplus, that economic growth, allows more loans to be issued in turn. So far, so good, perhaps. The very existence of money as we know it drives growth and so the linear 'take, make and dispose' economy is reinforced or led by the nose.

Growing populations and increasing numbers of middle class consumers worldwide are able to buy the products in sufficient numbers to keep this going, or at least until around the mid 1970s in the West, when employment in blue collar trades was increasingly shifted offshore, or removed by technological innovation. Additional purchasing power was needed as well as a general shift to employment in services since wages were no longer sufficient to buy the output of the economy. Both were stimulated by relaxing credit controls, and by falling commodity prices and final product prices, but at the cost of a series of asset bubbles culminating in the near collapse of the global financial system in 2007/08.

The linear economy sprang from our new found means of exploring the world, a scientific revolution and its 'world as machine' metaphor. Driven by money as debt into rapid and escalating growth it worked well so long as there were plentiful resources, especially energy, the 'master resource', plentiful sinks for wastes, and customers who could afford, one way or another, the products which were made. Driving for efficiency through labour productivity as a means of accelerating the economic machine brought ever larger profits, wages for those employed, and especially returns to capital. The means to purchase all the goods and services produced was never there, due to payments on interest which began to increasingly cycle in financial markets and which represented a bigger and bigger part of GDP in the last 25 years[10]. The linear economy began to falter as employment shifted, the new, well paid fulltime jobs became concentrated in financial services and niche occupations, the gap between better off and poor expanded. It's not a surprise, just a function of the system as it iterates. Meanwhile, other costs rose – from the impact of externalities, from welfare payments, from a falling ratio of workers to pensioners, from materials, energy and credit and interest costs to service assets (principally housing) and the consequent waste of human potential in unemployment, especially among the young.

Seen in this perspective, the golden generations of those in adulthood in Europe between 1950 and 1979 and in the credit expansion phase between 1979 and 2008 were enjoying a linear economy as good as it (ever) gets. No particular blame is being attached, rather it is a function of the system and its basic relationships between how the world is imagined to work (in a deterministic way, as discussed) and money, interest, materials, energy and efficiency in that period. After all, why wouldn't you, it was like finding the key to the candy store and blobbing out in the armchair – the incentives were pretty much all short term and narrow. The role of business was to exploit the game.

But what if there was another way of seeing the world, one based in the science of our times not in Newton's time, one which entrained systems in a virtuous cycle of capital building rather than in a vicious one where human, social, manufactured and natural capital are transformed into financial capital. Could we change the rules of the game? It's a rhetorical question and the answer is 'yes' and it's all pretty intuitive as it turns out. It's not a new idea, and has been rolling around in different forms for more than 30 years[11]. But what is different now is that it has been refined and has begun to engage business in a way that business recognises, and more importantly is core to understanding where prosperity might come from in a changing world.

"...individuals will not change their mode of thinking or operating within the world until their existing modes are proved beyond doubt, through direct experience, to be failing." Jake Chapman, *System Failure,* (2002)

It may be the case of 'come the necessity comes the invention', even if people like Walter R Stahel have been advocating it since the late 1970s (see Chapter 4). The timing needed to be right. Much has changed which makes this decade the gateway to the circular economy, much of it detailed above and summarised by the phrase "which way out?". It would be wrong to say that humans have come to their senses, it may be that only now do the advantages seem so clear. Perhaps a little run through of the basics first.

The old framework was that the world was machine like. It was deterministic, if you could only find the building blocks and the relationships you could describe the system accurately, or as close enough that it made no difference. In other words, cause and effect writ large, with enough effort it could all be understood. The whole is the sum of the parts. Except it isn't, not in most real world systems. That's the rub. The effects of feedback in systems with no fixed initial conditions, and many variables has led to an entire area of study called complexity theory[12]. These systems exhibited non-linearity. A certain input might have a disproportionate output and systems at a certain level of complexity might exhibit new emergent properties. The coming of the computer allowed humankind to model these dynamic systems. Before that the mathematics were complex and laborious to do and the relevance seemed low if the mechanical is assumed to be the general case. One of the first models was Jay Forrester's work, which became the basis of *Limits to Growth* in 1972, with its multiple scenarios around population and resources.

This all might remain something of a 'so-what?' curiosity but for the realisation that:

"The ability to study the order of intertwined and mutual causality in real-world systems opens up a new scientific realm. This could not be approximately done using either of today's mainstay approaches: mechanics (simple linear causality) or statistics (weakly connected causality). The vast majority of real-life natural, social and economic phenomena belong to the realm of complexity. Indeed, natural systems, whether physical, social or economic, only rarely exhibit simple causality or weakly connected causality." Sally Goerner, *After the Clockwork Universe: The Emerging Science and Culture of Integral Society* (1999)

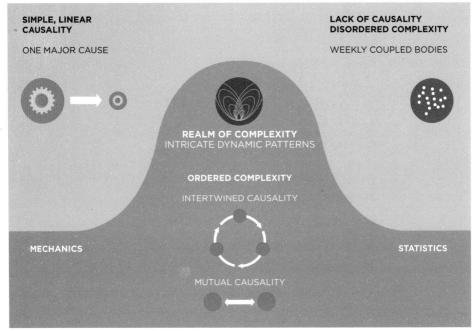

Figure 4 **The realm of complexity**[13]

Here is a useful diagram which shows the mechanical (linear) and statistical (disordered complexity) as very much in the tail of the distribution of systems overall. The conclusion is obvious, the complex iterative system is the general case, often termed 'ordered complexity'. It is the name of the game and as Gunter Pauli notes, "thinking in systems and cycles we become metabolists".

The metabolism. Perfect. Since George Lakoff reminds us that most thought is unconscious and almost all abstract thinking is metaphorical[14] then it seems appropriate for the metabolism to be one of the new core metaphors: it relates to the most elegant of complex systems, life itself. It replaces the machine metaphors, not as a trendy choice but because it better reflects the emerging scientific understanding we have about how the universe works. Because it better models how economies work and that in turn must confer advantages to practitioners – business.

Ordered, complex, intertwined mutually interdependent systems are the new normal. That is where the economy and business exist, and hence the notion that a circular economy is an expression of systems thinking: an opportunity to upgrade our economics and business to match an expanded, richer vision (as the cartoon in Figure 5 suggests). Brutally, it is to say business in the real world.

Figure 5 **'Desert island'**
(xkcd webcomic) http://xkcd.com/731/

And what that means in practice is the subject of many of the contributions to this reader. Key amongst them is the idea of capital maintenance connected to effective flows discussed by Walter R Stahel (see Chapter 4), fractal relationships discussed by Sally Goerner (See Chapter 8) in the context of free enterprise and entrepreneurship and the size of the prize as outlined by the Ellen MacArthur Foundation's reports *Towards the Circular Economy* (see Chapter 3). All assume a regenerative economy, an embedded economy.

Nobel Laureate Elinor Ostrom explained it this way in *Governing the Commons*: "Resource systems are best thought of as stock variables that are capable, under favorable conditions, of producing a maximum quantity of a flow variable without harming the stock or the resource system itself."

The challenge for business is how to thrive while materials are being endlessly transformed (where they are food for biological and technical cycles) using mostly current solar income and while stocks are rebuilt and/or maintained and abundance, elegantly enjoyed is the aim.

Notes

1 *Homo economicus, a rational fellow who weighs up the sum of his marginal utility, more a feature of the model than anyone corporeal who has ever existed*

2 *See, for example: http://press.princeton.edu/titles/7609.html. From this link you can download Chapter 1 of* Postmodern Moments in Modern Economics *by David F Ruccio and Jack Amariglio, Princeton University Press, (2003). "Modernism is not only an exhausted project, but a destructive one. One form of damage is its silencing of theoretical disagreement under the rubric of the unity of science and 'correct' scientific protocols. This has led to disdain for, neglect of, and hostility towards nonmainstream thought." (p4)*

3 *George Carlin said: "It was called the American Dream because you had to be asleep to believe it."*

4 *Every generation except the current one has seen rising living standards for the past 150 years (USA)*

5. *Steven Reid, Mythbusters: Strivers vs Skivers, article can be found at: www.neweconomics.org*

6. *For further information, visit http://www.mckinsey.com/insights/asia-pacific/meet_the_chinese_consumer_of_2020*

7 *See, for example: http://www.youtube.com/watch?v=eaf_btkvK6M or: http://www.theguardian.com/business/economics-blog/2012/mar/02/oil-prices-10-reasons-to-be-fearful*

8 *The difference between discoveries and production of conventional oil* has presaged an output plateau. (*NB. Conventional does not include natural gas liquids, an often confusing element in discussions about production in recent years.) To download the 'Oil Report' from October 2007, visit: www.energywatchgroup.org*

9 *Steve Keen,* Debunking Economics – Revised and Expanded Edition: The Naked Emperor Dethroned? *Zed Books, London (2011)*

10 *See: http://www.epi.org/blog/fiscal-implications-rising-capital-share-income/*

11 *See, for example, Kenneth Boulding and Walter R Stahel*

12 *Peter Senge is a well-known business consultant who has made use of systems thinking. He is author of* The Fifth Discipline: The Art and Practice of the Learning Organisation. *Also of note is the economist Eric Beinhocker, author of* The Origin of Wealth

13 *Figure adapted from Sally Goerner,* After the Clockwork Universe: The Emerging Science and Culture of Integral Society *(1999)*

14 *George Lakoff and Mark Johnson,* Philosophy in the Flesh: The Embodied Mind and Its Challenge to Western Thought *(1999)*

A CONCISE GUIDE TO THE CIRCULAR ECONOMY
KNOWING THE TERRITORY, SURVIVING AND THRIVING

2

Ken Webster

This chapter characterises the main differences between a linear and circular economy as systems. In so doing it points towards the opportunities and constraints for businesses that are seeking to take advantage of the transition or those trying to decide whether their current activities and business models are likely to thrive, or indeed to survive.

Ken Webster is Head of Innovation, Ellen MacArthur Foundation. He is a major contributor to the development of ideas around the circular economy. As Honorary Teaching Fellow at Bradford University School of Management he teaches on the Innovation, Enterprise and Circular Economy MBA.

ken.webster@ellenmacarthurfoundation.org

Ellen MacArthur Foundation
www.ellenmacarthurfoundation.org

A football game is an example of a system: it has some components, some rules for interaction, some boundaries and a goal. Infinite permutations of interaction proceed and the game can evolve, too, by negotiations over the rules, but by and large, a team introducing a rugby ball or a hockey stick is potentially disruptive and perhaps even destructive of the game.

Economies are a bit like football, a game with some rules: laws of contract, acceptable fiat money, contributions to the referees and the greater good (taxes), the following of health and safety regulation. There is a playing field: the idea of markets and competition for goals, often around wealth accumulation. There is an understanding of it, currently, that it is a throughput economy, a game of capital conversion where resources described as natural capital or social capital are converted into financial capital. In physical terms, forest, fishery, soil and mineral is mined for processing into goods and services. What people have traditionally done for themselves is transferred into what individuals purchase in the marketplace or sell, in terms of their daily labour. Land has been 'simplified' by the reduction of other species on it in the search for efficiency in farming. While fisheries have been simplified by the use of bigger nets and sonar and incentives which give little concern for by-catch. The benefits of the process circulate as a flow of income to various sectors of society. Benefitting from large surpluses through the deployment of cheap fossil fuel energy, we have reduced the amount of hard physical labour required and created, on the face of it, a cornucopia of products and opportunities, not to mention the ability to support 7 billion persons, if we wish. But it is a system, nonetheless, with a history and a number of entrainments: things which follow, connected characteristics at a big picture level, just as night follows day.

To explain: increasing scale offers lower costs and potentially more leverage or power in the marketplace. Mass production drives down the use of labour through energetic and technological substitutions and disruptions, while creating new occupations for some and increased income for those that remain.

Mass production demands mass consumption and ever more of both to guarantee the loans which will be made and the interest which is to be paid on money supplied to both. Mass consumption needs affordable and plentiful credit.

The competitive edge is often gained by cutting costs or rejecting responsibility for them. That vital juncture, the point of sale, offers a means of transferring responsibility to the buyer. Or, in the case of environmental damage, to the commons.

As markets become more saturated, attention is paid to planning in obsolescence and selling novelty, or selling brand and lifestyle and the shopping experience as much as product: churning the market. The interests of the consumer are bent to those of the throughput 'take, make and dispose' economy – out of necessity given the functioning of the system. As many costs as can be exported in dealing with waste are exported. There is also degradation of the social network from citizens to consumers, who must exist as ever disappointed and restless individuals[1] needing further purchases.

In the throughput economy the flow through of materials and energy is deemed essential – to economic growth, and behind that to the repayment of loans advanced ahead of production plus interest and creating the basis for further loans. But it is bought at an increasingly hard to bear cost. The preferences of consumer, producer and government are not aligned but there appear to be few modern alternatives. Certainly we can discard for now the aspirations to return to a craft society and the backbreaking toil of the past or imagining that a spontaneous moderation of consumption will occur which would coincide with decisions to raise the living standards of the poorest. The only choice is more economic growth which effectively means more of everything: more substitution of capital and machines for labour, efficiencies which enter the service industries and now affect the middle classes; more income for those who earn from interest against those who pay it, as debt builds up; more exploitation of ever poorer (even if substantial) energy and materials reserves.

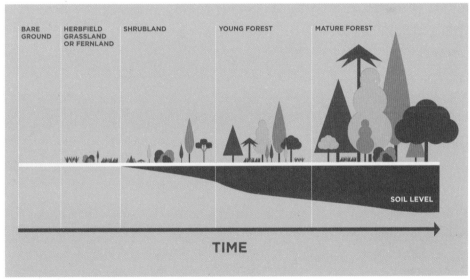

Figure 1 **Forest succession**

Economic growth in this model is best when there is lots of surplus. By analogy, it is like the forest which springs up again after fire makes a clearing, eager for sunlight and abundant soil nutrients and able to compete by reproducing quickly, a so called 'r' stage (see Figure 2) in the forest succession. As the canopy closes and the surplus accumulated in the soils is used up, the rules of the forest change, the balance of winners and losers shifts in concord (see Figure 2).

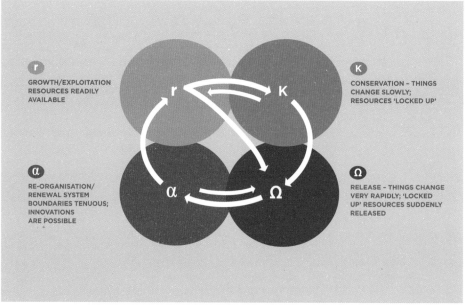

Figure 2 **The full adaptive cycle – key to a circular economy. Alpha through omega via r stage (rapid growth) and K (maturity into old age)**

A circular economy is a variation on the economic game, however the way in which it works, as a whole, its sets of interconnecting conditions, or rules, are seemingly familiar but produce very different outcomes. In the analogy of the forest (see Figure 1), the circular economy is perhaps closest to a dynamic 'K' system (see Figure 2), a mature forest which evolves from the new circumstances at the end of the 'r' stage. At 'K' stage plant and animal species exploit the granularity of the local conditions, the niches which open up and small additional nutrient and energy flows which are revealed. At the 'K' stage it is also as much about cooperation as competition between and within species since resources must cascade through many uses. Life, in the absence of surplus, forces together unlikely bedfellows for mutuality. It is a system of increased complexity and subtlety as time goes on. The winners are the ones who fit the system once again but the fit is not dominance through reproductive speed and fast growth. How could it be? It substitutes that which fits the system best for survival of the fittest individual (the strongest). But nothing lasts forever, as evidenced by the omega (nutrient release) and alpha stages (innovation and change, as shown in Figure 2).

In a circular economy there are assumed to be clean materials/'nutrients' flows, the biological materials/'nutrients' pathways, non toxic and connected so that capital, whether soils or fisheries, is restored: and the technical or human invented materials/'nutrients' pathways (see Figure 4 in chapter 3 for detail). These latter materials are kept in a separate pathway outside of the biosphere as far as possible while allowing for the inevitable decay and losses suffered by all things. Coherence has a price. It has to be paid, whether in renewable or fossil energy flows. So, these technical materials are designed for remanufacture, refurbishment or replacement at as high a state of quality or coherence as possible. Again the idea is that stocks are maintained and flows enabled which are as leak free as possible. The emphasis is on materials flows and the use, not consumption of technical materials. By contrast, biological materials for rebuilding through the biosphere flow in a measured way to enable the scavenging of the benefits of increasing decay or falling coherence in a clear non-toxic pathway. As a general guide, however, 'waste is food'.

The entrainment of a circular economy is very different to the linear economy. First of all the reasons why it should be circular are that with raw materials price, and energy volatility, it is a risk reducing strategy to establish a means of recovering products, components and, eventually, those technical materials in a low grade/incoherent state. It can also turn out to be very profitable (see Chapter 3). Increasingly, the challenge in mature markets is to tie in loyalty with users rather than separate the product, the responsibility and the materials from the business chain and take the risk of connection through sales alone. Mature markets have customers who are increasingly interested in machines – basic utilities, especially white goods, telephones, even vehicles – that 'just work', are reliable, and 'not their problem.' As Walter R Stahel notes, the 'tools' not the 'toys'.

The customers want the service, the performance rather than the product. The formerly externalised costs and the desire to 'churn' the products is replaced by design and performance which internalises these costs and drives them into being internalised benefits: in a service contract, extra profit comes from improving reliability and performance via upgrades and guaranteeing very low failure rates. This also cuts down the amount of waste that municipal bodies have to deal with, further cutting 'externalities' and regulatory costs.

As the flow matters in a different sense than previously – it is circular as far as materials go – additional materials are drawn into use from former waste stockpiles and the energy demands of a refurbishment or remanufactured pathway are significantly lower, so providing relief from rising energy prices and operating on reduced or more slowly rising energy demand, at least in the more mature economies. Regionally and locally, employment is expected to rise in an ever more service-orientated economy. Entire new industries with strong employment potential can arise, especially in dealing with local biological nutrient flows – decomposition, biogas, composting, urban food production, which had hitherto been waste flows – and very often smaller or medium scales. Or simply unprofitable (see Lufa Farms[2]).

Customer (user), producer (service provider) and government interests are more clearly aligned by the operation of markets under changing 'rules of the game'. If the throughput economy becomes a vicious spiral of decline when past its peak (since if it cannot grow it goes into reverse by process of positive reinforcement – a debt deflationary spiral – see Table 1), then the circular economy might be a virtuous cycle as it (re)builds all capitals and internalises costs as it proceeds. However, the circularity 'rules' extend beyond the mechanics of production to the question of prices, costs and the money system.

The market is useful to rational decision-making when prices are conveying accurate messages about costs. The internalisation of costs in a circular economy helps this accurate pricing, as does a shift to ensure consistency between tax and spend policies and the kind of economy which has evolved or is desired. At present the throughput economy supports the replacement of labour by technology (and cheap energy) by taxing income and writing off much capital depreciation in tax terms. This would be inconsistent with a circular economy as labour is a plentiful and renewable resource, which we wish to encourage the use of and it is vital to the success of a circular economy, as it is more dependent on service relationships and more materials handling at different scales. Taxes could focus on the non renewable, on unearned income and on waste streams.

Simply eliminating the subsidies applied to the exploitation of many primary resources – in fossil fuels, mining, forestry, agriculture, fishing and banking – would enable prices to better reveal full costs. The money system (as noted) also drives a linear economy, because money created as debt promotes competition to earn enough to repay, plus interest, and is only possible by assuring the system that it is growing exponentially. More production will guarantee the payments of compound interest and back the new loans.

Money issued debt free is possible as is the flurry of interest in the development of complementary currencies to bring diversity and flexibility and to energise exchange. To keep money in circulation, a form of 'holding fee' (negative interest) for large balances of money is being mooted by Bernard Lietaer and others[3]. It is claimed to be a way of encouraging longer term investment, something very necessary for a durable economy built on regeneration and/or maintenance of stocks. After all, if positive interest drives the linear economy, a mirror of this might be consistent with a circular economy.

Summary

There follows in Table 1 an attempt to contrast linear and circular modes for the general elucidation of the idea that systems entrain and the consequences are just that - consequences - and much less a matter of choice at an individual level than might be supposed. It surely beholds us, if extending and exploiting circularity in business is the aim, to know what we are involved in and how a subtle change of the rules of the game (whether brought by changing technologies and other dynamics) might have far reaching consequences over time.

Table 1 is a characterisation of different systems and their consequences. There is nothing here about explicit social policy or political systems. Business always expects to work under whatever political layering is applied in a country. A circular economy can work under a whole range of arrangements. However, one assumes that there is reason to suggest that it would be encouraging of and work more readily where individual aspirations for democracy, free association, prosperity and independent living in functioning and diverse communities are valued. In character, a circular econmy is evidently more likely to point to a variety of scales, be more connected, participatory and likely to balance competition and cooperation, if only because resource and energy constraints push it that way and, curiously, because of how our brains work.

A whole systems aesthetic is likely to exercise the empathetic neural pathways[4]. These pathways are key learning pathways which relate to how others experience situations, but like all neural pathways they need exercise – use – to be effective contributors. These pathways are exercised more often in a circular economy context because understanding and working with suppliers and customers in ways which are aimed at increasing effective flows requires taking on others' points of view: common standards, cooperation, co-working and more 'open source' approaches. A sensitivity to the bigger picture, including the interdependence exhibited in systems approaches is obvious. Cognitive scientists, such as George Lakoff and others, point to the empathetic neural pathways as operating as a counterpoint to the more 'selfish' and materialistic or focussed pathways more commonly applied – or simply more appropriate for success in a linear economy. After all, a different mode of thinking or a mindset is just that – different – and the character and place of business in relation to society is likely to be different too, simply by entrainment generated by the system.

Table 1 **Characterisation of linear and circular economies and their consequences**

Linear	Circular	Notes
Externalises costs in search of production cost reduction	Internalises costs in search for quality service/ performance and low risk	Refers to manufactures like white goods of medium complexity, especially those with reasonable use periods
POS = point of sale and ends most responsibility	Usually rent/lease/recovery but business extends responsibility. POS = point of service	If biological pathway assumes non-toxic "waste = food" consumption via appropriate cascading
Creates waste streams for municipalities and individuals to deal with	Reduces waste streams and provides value streams instead	Might reduce GDP as this does not distinguish between 'goods' and 'bads' in its calculation
Promotes global scale in production to secure low costs and market position	Regional and local scales feasible as value is more in the service provided than the selling of product	Note changing approaches to manufactures – e.g. devolved digital manufacturing
Encourages standardisation to add to efficiency/ease of consumption	Encourages standardisation of components and protocols to encourage repair, recovery and reuse	Open source – download designs not ship products
Consumption turnover encouraged – planned obsolescence etc. Possession trumps access	User mentality, trouble free service or performance sought (reliability). Less turnover. Access trumps possession	Huge opportunity for marketeers to profit from this
Economic growth driven by compound interest and money as debt	Investing in restorative long-term schemes driven by complementary currencies, negative interest, money issued debt free	Reverses the effect of net present value calculations
Prices reflect only the private costs of production distribution, sale etc.	Prices reflect the full costs aided by reduction of externalised costs	

Table ©Ellen MacArthur Foundation/Ken Webster 2013

Linear	Circular	Notes
Tax on labour encourages labour productivity (substitute capital or energy). Reduces employment if growth not strong	Taxes off income and other renewables and on waste, non-renewables, unearned income. Increases employment generally	
Recycling represents another raw material flow and ignores lost embodied energy and quality	Recycling represents a low grade option – an outer loop. Sometimes necessary	Recycling legitimises a linear economy by promising what it cannot possibly achieve – a closed loop on short-cycle, low-value materials
Transforms natural and social capital into financial capital via a short-term preference – rapid, large flows	(Re)builds capital (stocks) from which to derive more and better flows over the longer term	Assumes in circular economy that natural and social capital are degraded at starting point
As the throughput model externalises costs there is a truncated materials flow to concern the product designers	As the product and service are wholly dependent on a functioning materials flow which is 'closed loop' the 'fit' is imperative. Whole systems design indicated	
Economic growth evolves to become a need to offset labour productivity and to meet interest payments	Economic growth replaced by more sophisticated measure: assumes increasing prosperity and well being as part of a restorative cycle	A long standing discussion
Production> sale in a linear system can be very competitive for product sales and market share in the context of need for low costs and thus economies of scale, often global [supply push for branded products]	Whole systems design is inherently more 'we' than 'me' orientated. Cooperation will be required as well as competition. Markets, regional or local, perhaps more differentiated [demand pull for generic products]	
Basic metaphor is 'world as machine and parts'. Humans can understand predict and control. Individual is centre of the world and can work instrumentally to achieve ever greater results	Basic metaphor is of living systems –'metabolisms' – where we have complex relationships in which we are participants, have influence and limited opportunity to understand (we need to review frequently)	The general case is one where the system is non-linear, the special or less common case is the linear

Notes

1 *If the customer is satisfied, the next sale is progressively harder to make*

2 *Profitable urban farming, see: https://lufa.com/en*

3 *See, for example: http://www.telegraph.co.uk/finance/economics/9895068/Bank-of-England-mulls-negative-interest-rates.html or, for a detailed discussion, see Bernard Lietaer, author, financial expert, and co-designer of the ECU (the monetary mechanism that later became the euro), http://www.clubofrome.org/?p=4478*

4 *On the basis of George Lakoff and Mark Johnson's work described as 'embodied realism', see their book:* Philosophy in the Flesh: The Embodied Mind and Its Challenge to Western Thought. *Basic Books (1999)*

3

*Ellen MacArthur Foundation with
analytics by McKinsey & Company*

An illustrated summary of the size of the prize as seen
through the lens of the Foundation and its knowledge
partner analysts. This chapter focuses on fast moving
consumer goods globally but extends more widely.

Analysis and diagrams initially published in Towards the Circular Economy 1 and 2.

Over the period October 2011 to January 2013 the Ellen MacArthur Foundation engaged in assessing the answer to three crucial questions about a circular economy:

1. Can a circular economy model decouple resources and growth?
2. Is it profitable for business?
3. Is it good for the economy?

To support them, business consultants McKinsey & Company provided in depth analysis. The outcomes are the reports *Towards the Circular Economy*, Volumes 1 and 2. Although the general idea of a circular economy is not entirely new (Chapter 1) it has come into focus as an attempted answer to a basic question facing the world's economy in these years. At the end of an era of cheap energy, readily available materials and expansive consumer credit, the question is 'Which Way Out?' This is the question to ask where markets are often saturated and there is evidence of jobless growth – where growth exists at all following the financial crash of 2008 and the subsequent Great Recession. The question is not just relevant to business of course but it is especially relevant to business, since the challenge of the end of a predominately linear economy is profound and affects many, if not most, business models.

With a linear economy being built for throughput, a switch to 'roundput' is not trivial. Further, the relationship of business to the systems of supply, the relationship with customers and the financial markets is changed too. Even if much of an economy is built on services rather than manufacturing and food and farming or raw material extraction, the question remains. The circular economy makes the business case – for example – for a shift from consumption to use for many categories of durables and of designing out waste; for novel forms of collaboration and different transport networks. A circular economy is not over in the manufacturing corner. It's an economy not a sector which is at stake. The good news is that the outlines of a circular economy can be seen, and would go a long way towards decoupling growth and resources. It is good for the economy and it is capable of very large materials costs savings, so good for business too. In short, there is a prize and it is substantial.

The Foundation reports came out at about the time other reports reiterated the possibilities of savings by going towards renewables in the energy sector: *Renewable Energy Matters*[1] and *RE-thinking 2050* by the European Renewable Energy Council[2]. The Rocky Mountain Institute's publication *Reinventing Fire*[3] combined these reports – also stressing the costs savings and return on investment – to document the basis for a more prosperous world economy with substantial employment and tax benefits.

Here is an illustrated summary of the size of the prize as seen through the lens of the Foundation and its analysts. This summary focuses on the fast moving consumer goods globally but extends more widely. Figure 1 shows some of the pressures in the sector.

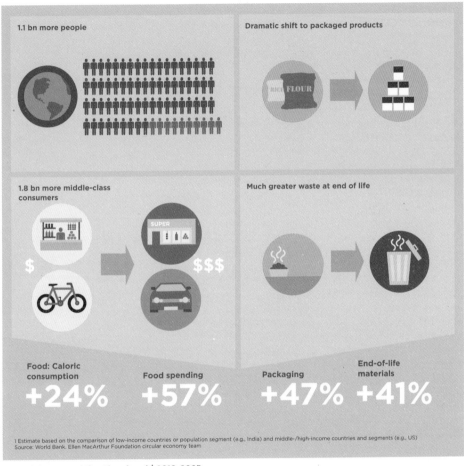

Figure 1 **A consumption time bomb**[1] 2010-2025

The last 150 years of industrial evolution have been dominated by a one-way or linear model of production and consumption in which goods are manufactured from raw materials, sold, used, and then discarded as waste. This model has been exceptionally successful in providing affordable products to consumers and material prosperity to billions. In developed economies, it has largely displaced a traditional economy that featured more reuse and regeneration but required more labour and produced lower returns on investment.

While there is still room for the linear model to expand geographically and realise even higher efficiencies, there are signs that the coming decades will require productivity gains and quality improvements at a new order of magnitude. As the global middle class more than doubles in size to nearly 5 billion by 2030, consumption and material intensity will rise accordingly, driving up input costs and price volatility at a time when access to new resource reserves is becoming more challenging and expensive. Perhaps most troubling is that this sudden surge in demand may have adverse effects on the environment that further constrain supply. Symptoms of these constraints are currently most visible in the food and water supply. Declines in soil fertility are already estimated to cost around USD 40 billion globally.

Modern circular and regenerative forms of consumption – so far limited to a few high-end categories – represent a promising alternative and are gaining ground. Powerful examples of their economic viability at scale exist today, from anaerobic digestion (AD) of household waste to apparel recovery. While these examples are still limited in geographical scope, we estimate the full potential of the circular economy to be as much as USD 700 billion in global consumer goods materials savings alone. Our product- and country-level analyses covered examples in product categories that represent 80% of the total consumer goods market by value, namely food, beverages, textiles, and packaging. Highlights of opportunities for profitable businesses include the following:

• **Household food waste.** An income stream of USD 1.5 billion[4] could be generated annually for municipalities and investors by collecting household food waste in the UK separately and processing it in line with circular principles to generate biogas and return nutrients to agricultural soils. If all countries in the EU matched Italy's high rates of separate collection of household food waste for biogas and compost production, the resulting income stream would give towns and cities a new source of revenue.

• **Industrial beverage processing waste.** An additional profit of USD 1.90 to 2.00 per hectolitre of beer produced could be created in Brazil on top of the margin for beer by selling the biggest waste product, brewer's spent grains, to farmers in the fish farming (specifically tilapia) and livestock sectors, thus 'cascading' it to another industry as a feed supplement. Cascaded uses are relevant for many food processing by-products.

• **Clothing.** A revenue of USD 1,975 per tonne of clothing collected could be generated in the UK if the garments were sold at current prices, with the gross profit of USD 1,295 comfortably outweighing the cost of USD 680 required to collect and sort each tonne. Like Italy in household food waste collection, the UK sets a standard worth emulating, with an average clothing collection rate of 65% of clothes discarded.

• **Packaging.** A cost reduction of 20% from USD 29 to USD 24 per hectolitre of beer consumed would be possible in the UK by shifting from disposable to reusable glass beer bottles, which would lower the cost incurred for packaging, processing, and distribution. While durability would require a 34% increase in the amount of glass used per bottle, this increase in material would be dwarfed by the savings that accrue from being able to reuse such bottles up to 30 times, as currently achieved in Germany.

Over time, the market is likely to systematically reward companies with an edge in circular business practices and hence dramatically lower resource requirements. With new technologies in hand, they can win by scaling up the concept of the circular economy. There will also be rewards in rapidly urbanising countries where waste streams of nutrients, heat, partially treated waste water or CO_2 can be converted back into high-value biological products or energy using much shorter and more resilient supply chains. The time to invest in building a circular economy is now.

The success – and limits – of linear consumption
Between 1900 and 2000, global GDP grew 20 times and created hitherto unknown levels of material prosperity. The availability of consumer goods of increasing quality and reliability at ever-lower cost was supported by new production technologies, globalised supply chains, fewer labour inputs, and what we call a 'linear' industrial economy. Within this linear model, resources are extracted from the earth for production and consumption on a one-way track with no plans for reuse or active regeneration of the natural systems from which they have been taken. In developed economies, the linear economy has largely displaced the traditional 'lower productivity' circular economy.

The linear economy is material and energy intensive; it relies on economies of scale, and typically builds on complex and international supply chains. All these supply chains have a common goal – the consumer. The goods an OECD citizen buys for consumption annually – 800 kg of food and beverages, 120 kg of packaging, and 20 kg of new clothing and shoes – are, for the most part, not returned for any further economic use. In the current 'take, make and dispose' system, around 80% of these materials will end up in incinerators, landfill or waste water. They come to a dead end.

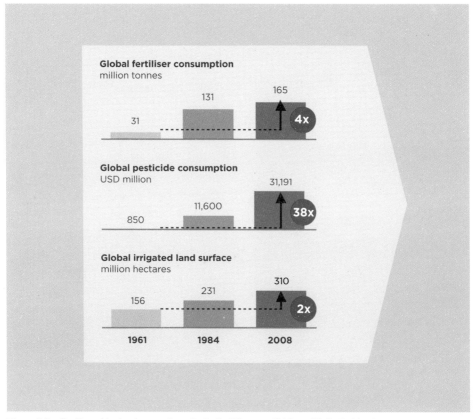

Figure 2 **Application of technology and products: fertiliser, pesticide and irrigated land**

There is still room to expand the linear economy model geographically to the developing world, where labour and capital are not yet organised around agricultural or processing value chains optimised for efficiency. At the same time, there are growing signs that the power of the linear model is reaching a limit:

• In modern manufacturing processes, opportunities to increase efficiency still exist, but the gains are largely incremental and insufficient to generate real competitive advantage or differentiation.

• Manufacturers' margins are being compressed by slow growth in demand, increasing costs, and higher price volatility for resources.

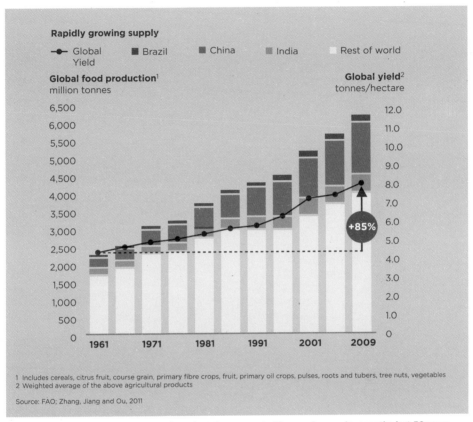

Rapidly growing supply

—●— Global Yield ■ Brazil ■ China ■ India ▢ Rest of world

Global food production[1]
million tonnes

Global yield[2]
tonnes/hectare

+85%

1961 1971 1981 1991 2001 2009

1 Includes cereals, citrus fruit, course grain, primary fibre crops, fruit, primary oil crops, pulses, roots and tubers, tree nuts, vegetables
2 Weighted average of the above agricultural products

Source: FAO; Zhang, Jiang and Ou, 2011

Figure 3 **Application of technology and products has generated impressive results over the last 50 years**

• Agricultural productivity is growing more slowly than ever before, and soil fertility and even the nutritional value of foods are declining.

• The risks to food security and safety associated with long, 'hyper-optimised' global supply chains appear to be increasing.

For these reasons, alternative models for production, distribution, and consumption based on reusing resources and regenerating natural capital have caught the attention of businesses around the world. 'Circular' sources of value appear more transformational and less incremental than further efficiency improvements.

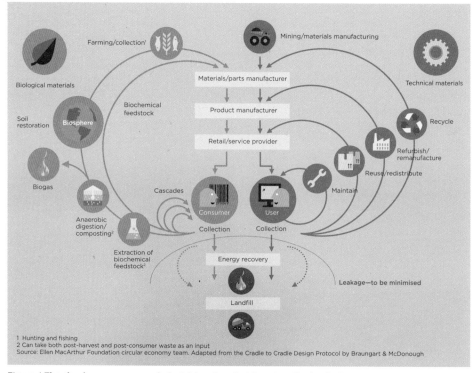

Figure 4 **The circular economy – an industrial system that is restorative by design**

Rediscovering a circular model

For durables, the benefits of reuse have been widely demonstrated. For consumer goods – such as food and beverages or apparel and their packaging – which are short-lived and often transformed during use, the economic benefits of a circular design are more complex in origin and harder to assess.

We estimate the total material value of fast-moving consumer goods at USD 3.2 trillion. Currently, we recover an estimated 20% of this material, largely through decomposition (cascading of waste and by-products through adjacent supply chains, returning nutrients to the soil, and recycling) and partly through reuse. In the future, we believe that a much higher share of consumer goods materials could potentially be recovered though reuse and decomposition. Even in the near term, without the dramatic application of bio-based products and the full redesign of supply chains, the value that can be recovered could be increased to 50%.

Recovering part of the USD 2.6 trillion of material value lost today is a huge opportunity for fast-moving consumer goods companies. However, they face significant hurdles as they try to break out of the linear model. We need to build efficient collection systems to capture the materials value of goods that are consumed far from their point of origin, design better combinations of goods and packaging, and dramatically increase the attention management gives to recovering value in the post-use stages of the supply chain. Enough thriving examples of circular business models already exist today to give us confidence that these challenges can be met.

Commercial opportunities today
In our product-level analysis, we have studied specific examples in product categories that represent 80% of the total consumer goods market by value: food, beverages, textiles, and packaging. Circular opportunities exist all along the value chain: in manufacturing (food and beverages), in the distribution and consumption stages (textiles, packaging), and in post-use processing (food waste). Generally, in developing countries, more circular opportunities are lost at the manufacturing stage. In developed countries, losses are more heavily concentrated at the consumer level.

Food and beverages
There are profitable ways to deal with the mixed food waste discarded by households and the hospitality sector. In the UK, processing this waste in line with circular principles could generate an income stream of USD 1.5 billion annually – providing a major economic opportunity for both municipalities and investors while generating biogas and returning nutrients to agricultural soils.

There is further potential for circularity in industrial food processing, where waste is mostly created as a by-product – such as brewer's spent grains in beer-making or orange peel in juice production – with beer – the world's third most-popular beverage after water and tea, and representative of foods and beverages that generate valuable processing by-products – keeping brewer's spent grains out of landfill. Instead, selling them as a feed supplement in accordance with circular principles can create a profit of USD 1.90 per hectolitre of beer produced.

Clothing
There are profitable circular opportunities to reuse end-of-life clothing, which, in addition to being worn again, can also be cascaded down to other industries to make insulation or stuffing, or simply recycled into yarn to make fabrics that save virgin fibres. If sold at current prices in the UK, a tonne of collected and sorted clothing can generate a revenue of USD 1,975, or a gross profit of USD 1,295 after subtracting the USD 680 required to collect and sort each tonne. We also see an opportunity in expanding the 'clothing-for-hire' segment to everyday clothes, as another offshoot of the asset-light trend.

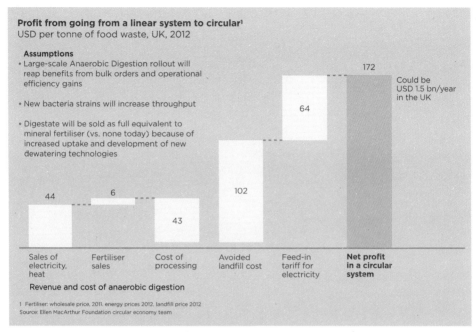

Profit from going from a linear system to circular[1]
USD per tonne of food waste, UK, 2012

Assumptions
- Large-scale Anaerobic Digestion rollout will reap benefits from bulk orders and operational efficiency gains
- New bacteria strains will increase throughput
- Digestate will be sold as full equivalent to mineral fertiliser (vs. none today) because of increased uptake and development of new dewatering technologies

172

Could be USD 1.5 bn/year in the UK

64

102

44   6

43

| Sales of electricity, heat | Fertiliser sales | Cost of processing | Avoided landfill cost | Feed-in tariff for electricity | **Net profit in a circular system** |

Revenue and cost of anaerobic digestion

1 Fertiliser: wholesale price, 2011. energy prices 2012. landfill price 2012
Source: Ellen MacArthur Foundation circular economy team

Figure 5 **Shifting to a circular system for food waste could create profits of USD 172 per tonne of food waste**

Packaging

Recovery for reuse, keeping packaging in circulation longer, will deliver dramatically greater materials savings and profit than the traditional linear one-way system, especially if collection rates are high. Our modelling of beer containers shows that shifting to reusable glass bottles would lower the cost of packaging, processing, and distribution by approximately 20% per hectolitre of beer consumed.

Recovery for decomposition is another option. End-of-life materials can be cycled back through one of two forms: either recycling the materials or returning nutrients to the soil via biodegradable packaging.

Recycling – This is a solution when it is not feasible to install reuse infrastructure, but significant materials savings are immediately available by collecting and recycling used packaging. In OECD countries, prices of raw materials already make it profitable today for collection and recycling companies to increase the volume and range of the different fractions recycled. Our case shows a profit of nearly USD 200 per tonne of plastic collected for recycling. In parallel, more thoughtful product design and material choices should also significantly improve recovery and regeneration solutions.

Biodegradable packaging – This is the solution of choice when single-use packaging can facilitate the return of bio-based materials (e.g., food) back to the soil, or when no other viable end-of-life option exists. Most available biodegradable materials are currently more expensive than traditional packaging, but innovative solutions are being developed in specific applications and could allow the profitable evolution of biodegradable packaging.

Because they extract value from what are otherwise wasted resources, these and other examples of the modern circular economy are inherently more productive than linear business models. Technologies and regulatory solutions already exist to support businesses and investors in seizing such opportunities and changing consumption habits towards longer use and reuse. As Steve Sharp, executive director of marketing at Marks & Spencer, says: "Not many years ago people would have been incredulous at the idea of routinely recycling bottles and plastic, yet this is now commonplace behaviour. We want to try to achieve that same shift of behaviour with our Shwopping campaign and make recycling clothes a habit." M&S CEO Mark Bolland adds: "We're leading a change in the way we all shop for clothing, forever.[5]"

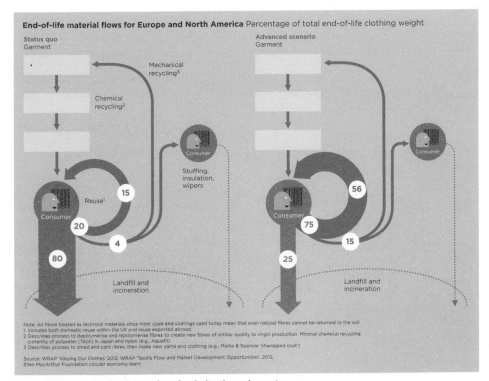

Figure 6 **Clothing: Further increasing circularity through greater collection and closed-loop recycling, both mechanical and chemical**

Accounting for business and economic benefits

The full value of these circular opportunities for fast-moving consumer goods could be as much as USD 700 billion per annum in material savings or a recurring 1.1% of 2010 GDP, all net of materials used in the reverse-cycle processes. Those materials savings would represent about 20% of the materials input costs incurred by the consumer goods industry. In addition, we expect the following benefits:

• *Innovation.* The aspiration to replace one-way products with goods that are 'circular by design' and create reverse logistics networks and other systems to support the circular economy is a powerful spur to new ideas. The benefits of a more innovative economy include higher rates of technological development; improved materials, labour, and energy efficiency, and more profit opportunities for companies.

• *Land productivity and soil health.* Land degradation costs an estimated USD 40 billion annually worldwide, without taking into account the hidden costs of increased fertiliser use, loss of biodiversity, and loss of unique landscapes. Higher land productivity, less waste in the food value chain, and the return of nutrients to the soil will enhance the value of land and soil as assets. The circular economy, by moving much more biological material through the anaerobic digestion or composting process and back into the soil, will reduce the need for replenishment with additional nutrients. This is the principle of regeneration at work.

• *Job creation potential.* A circular economy might bring greater local employment, especially in entry-level and semi-skilled jobs, which would address a serious issue facing the economies of developed countries.

This total prize is just the beginning of a much bigger set of transformative value-creation plays as the world scales up the new circular technologies and business models. We are likely to see a selective 'grafting' of new circular business models and technologies during this period of transition. Initially, these grafts may appear to be modest in their impact and play into niche markets (e.g., growing greenhouse tomatoes, hiring out high-end fashion items). But, over the next 15 years, these new business models will likely gain an increasing competitive advantage because they inherently create much more value from each unit of resource. In addition, they are likely to meet other market requirements, associated with more secure supply, more convenience for consumers, and lower environmental costs.

In a world of 9 or 10 billion consumers with fierce competition for resources, market forces are likely to favour those models that best combine specialised knowledge and cross-sector collaboration to create the most value per unit of resource over those models that simply rely on ever more resource extraction and throughput. Natural selection will likely favour the agile hybrids – able to quickly combine circularity with scale – that are best adapted to a planet transformed by humanity.

By 2030, the prize could be much more than USD 700 billion – and we expect to see circular business models accounting for a large part of the global bio-value chains. In that not-so-distant world, investors, managers, and regulators will be talking about how companies get going and start learning how to hybridise their business models – for markets that will be worth well over USD 25 trillion.

The shift has begun – mainstreaming the circular economy
Why now? Our economy currently seems locked into a system in which everything from production economics and contracts to regulation and the way people behave favours the linear model of production and consumption. However, this lock-in is weakening under the pressure of several powerful disruptive trends. First, resource scarcity and tighter environmental standards are here to stay. Their effect will be to reward circular businesses that extract value from wasted resources over 'take, make and dispose' businesses. Second, information technology is now so advanced that it can trace materials anywhere in the supply chain, identify products and material fractions, and track product status during use. Third, we are in the midst of a pervasive shift in consumer behaviour: a new generation of consumers seems prepared to prefer access over ownership.

Capturing the new opportunities will require leading corporations and municipal authorities to develop a new set of 'circular' muscles and capabilities along their traditional supply chains. These new capabilities will be reinforced by a set of fundamental developments in resource markets, technology and information systems, and consumer preferences:

• Urbanisation that centralises flows of consumer goods and waste streams;

• A set of new technologies (e.g., anaerobic digestion) that enables dramatic improvements in the way value is extracted from today's biological waste streams as well as opportunities to combine multiple waste streams (CO_2, heat, waste water, nutrients) into advanced agro-manufacturing systems;

• New IT capabilities that support more precise management and tracking and tracing of biological flows in the system (e.g., RFID chips that provide detailed information about product spoilage rates);

• Emergence of online retail channels that redefine the way value chains work in distribution, waste recovery, and consumer choice without increasing material impact;

• New business models that improve control over scarce resources and 'assetise' them for reuse in value-maximising transfers as feedstock to subsequent industrial or agricultural processes;

• A new model of collaborative consumerism – in which consumers embrace services that enable them to access products on demand rather than owning them – and collaborative consumption models that provide more interaction between consumers, retailers, and manufacturers (e.g., performance-for-pay models, rent or leasing schemes, return and reuse);

• New packaging technologies and systems that extend food life and minimise packaging waste.

Companies are successfully building more circular business models in and for the consumer goods industry, and we see new roles and vantage points emerging:

• *Volume aggregators:* Markets for residues and by-products are currently severely under-developed, creating arbitrage opportunities for volume aggregators who stand at the forefront of organising these markets. ASOS, an aspiring online 'fashion destination' that offers more than 850 brands of new clothes, has extended its scope to the reverse cycle by creating a parallel platform where consumers can resell end-of-life clothing, and small firms can market 'vintage' garments and accessories as well as new ones. More specialised companies offer sales platforms in the business-to-business environment, too, such as the Waste Producer Exchange (WPE) in the UK, which supports users in selling waste products and materials.

• *Technology pioneers:* New technologies, (such as PHA bioplastics production from industrial waste water) offer technology leaders a vast array of opportunities. A recent rush of private equity capital into recycling and circular technology may signal the first influx of semi-permanent settlers on this frontier. Veolia has pioneered the production of bioplastics from sludge.

Waste-water treatment systems today often use bacteria that eat sludge and neutralise it into carbon. Using proprietary technology, Veolia has achieved a breakthrough in converting this 'waste-water carbon' into biomass rich in PHA, which has mechanical properties equivalent to polypropylene and is thus valuable in making consumer plastics and chemicals. Veolia produced the first biopolymers from municipal waste in 2011, and is now refining the process to meet end-customer specifications at full-scale waste-water treatment sites in Belgium and Sweden.

• *Micro-marketeers:* In the food and beverage industry, large retailers such as Woolworths in Australia, WholeFoods in the US, and Migros in Switzerland, as well as global food giants such as Unilever, Nestlé, Danone, and Kraft Foods, are preparing for markets with more local sourcing, distributed manufacturing, increased customer interaction, diversified customer demand, multi-channel purchasing (including home delivery), and ultimately more intimate customer relationships. At the same time, low-cost same-day delivery services allow local brick-and-mortar companies to compete with national brands online, further propelled by the emergence of online 'hyper-local' advertising platforms that allow people to find such businesses in their neighbourhood. Serving these micro-markets at scale and developing an integrated 'systems' offering that links products, ordering, delivery, and aftersales service could be the name of the game, and could even feature 'assisted' self-production by the consumer. In such a strategy, the circular economy could become a major source of differentiation – if not an obligation. Micro-marketeers could proactively offer B2B service contracts, develop blueprints for 'zero-waste' plants, or establish food waste reuse centres.

• *Urban-loop providers:* Urbanisation in emerging economies will create urban and peri-urban systems where waste streams of nutrients, heat, partially treated waste water, or CO_2 are converted back into high-value biological products using much

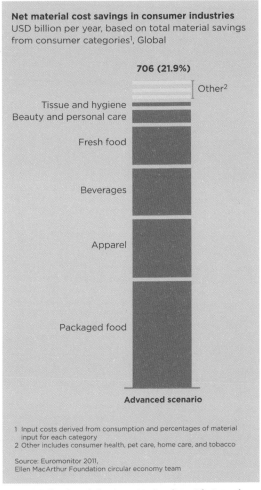

Net material cost savings in consumer industries
USD billion per year, based on total material savings
from consumer categories[1], Global

706 (21.9%)

Other[2]

Tissue and hygiene
Beauty and personal care

Fresh food

Beverages

Apparel

Packaged food

Advanced scenario

1 Input costs derived from consumption and percentages of material
  input for each category
2 Other includes consumer health, pet care, home care, and tobacco

Source: Euromonitor 2011,
Ellen MacArthur Foundation circular economy team

Figure 7 **Adoption of circular setup in relevant fast-moving consumer goods sectors could yield net material cost savings of USD 595 – 706 billion per year at a global level**

shorter and more resilient supply chains than today. Urban-loop economies offer a playing field for businesses with sophisticated know-how in design, engineering, and infrastructure operations. An example of this is The Plant, Chicago, a vertical aquaponic farm growing tilapia and vegetables that also serves as an incubator for craft food businesses and operates an anaerobic digester and a combined heat and power plant. Discarded materials from one business are used as a resource for another in an explicitly circular system.

• *Product-to-service converters:* In the textile industry, players like Patagonia – which pioneered the 'Common Threads Initiative' to reduce the environmental footprint of its garments – seek longer and more intimate customer relationships beyond the point of sale. Value-added offerings like repair, amendment, return and leasing offer much greater customer interaction at multiple touchpoints. Some players are beginning to redefine themselves as fashion or style partners with superior customer insights and value opportunities along the life cycle and across different categories.

We do not know how the shift will come about. It could come slowly or in a sudden sweep, as a reaction to external shocks. It may be the outcome of stirring public stimuli ('man on the moon') or of a killer application, as a silent manufacturing revolution. It could even emerge as grassroots consumer activism, or as voluntary, inclusive industry commitment. History has seen all of these patterns lead to breakthroughs: we do not know which of them will tip consumption into a more regenerative mode. We do expect, however, that the shift will play out between pioneering industry leaders, discriminating, well-informed consumers, and forward-looking public constituencies.

To support collaboration and knowledge transfer between companies engaged in implementing circular economy solutions, the Ellen MacArthur Foundation has created the Circular Economy 100, an invitational global platform for 100 pioneering businesses to accelerate the transition to a circular economy over a 1,000-day innovation period. The CE100 supports its members via a number of enabling initiatives, including: an online library of best practices, insights and learnings, acceleration workshops, an annual summit to showcase solutions and leading thinking, network and partnership opportunities with other CE100 members and universities, and executive education.

Notes

1 Renewable Energies Agency (Germany), http://www.renewables-in-germany.com

2 http://www.erec.org Brussels

3 Rocky Mountain Institute, http://www.rmi.org/ReinventingFire

4 Includes revenue from feed-in-tariff in the U.K. and avoided landfill fees

5 http://platform-online.net/2012/10/ms-unveil-first-shwopping-garment/

THE BUSINESS ANGLE OF A CIRCULAR ECONOMY
HIGHER COMPETITIVENESS, HIGHER RESOURCE SECURITY AND MATERIAL EFFICIENCY

4

Walter R Stahel

The present economy is not sustainable with regard to its per capita material consumption. A dematerialisation of the economy of industrialised countries can be achieved by a change in course, from an industrial economy built on throughput to a circular economy built on stock optimisation, decoupling wealth and welfare from resource consumption while creating more work. The business models of a circular economy have been known since the mid-1970s and are now applied in a number of industrial sectors.

Walter R Stahel is Founder-Director of The Product-Life Institute, Geneva and Head of Risk Management Research at Geneva Association (1987-2013). He is an alumni of ETH Zurich, Doctor Honoris Causa (University of Surrey, 2013) and Visiting Professor, Faculty of Engineering and Physical Sciences, University of Surrey.

wrstahel2014@gmail.com

The Product-Life Institute
www.product-life.org

Executive summary

A circular economy is about economics. However, it is characterised by a number of principles that do not exist in the linear industrial economy. As a result, policy-makers and economic actors of the manufacturing economy do not know them, nor their impact on the economy.

The principles ruling the circular economy include the following:

Principle 1
The smaller the loop (activity-wise and geographically) the more profitable and resource efficient it is.

Principle 2
Loops have no beginning and no end; value maintained replaces value added.

Principle 3
The speed of the circular flows is crucial; the efficiency of managing stock in the circular economy increases with a decreasing flow speed.

Principle 4
Continued ownership is cost efficient: reuse, repair and remanufacture without a change of ownership saves double transaction costs.

Principle 5
A circular economy needs functioning markets.

Compared to the linear manufacturing economy, the main impacts of a circular economy include:

- Reduction of virgin resource consumption and associated transports and environmental impairment, end of life waste volumes and associated transports and environmental impairment
- Substitution of manpower for energy and materials; 'caring' for fashion as driver; regional economy for global supply chain
- Conservation of embodied energy (grey energy), CO_2 emissions, water (virtual water).

The main focus is on conserving economic stocks, increasing their utilisation value and optimisation utilisation through an intelligent management of stocks. Managing stocks is already the norm for the following:
- Human labour (work), skills and experience
- Knowledge and wisdom
- Health and health care
- Natural capital (biodiversity, organic agriculture)
- Culture and cultural heritage.

The circular economy is extending the strategy of intelligent stock management to stocks of manufactured capital (human-made, physical goods) through, for instance, reuse and service-life extension of goods – remanufacturing means bringing used products to a like-new functional state with equivalent quality assurance.

A circular economy corresponds to the objectives of a 'green economy':
- Creating an innovation-focused national economy
- Promoting an economy in loops and closes local loops
- Reducing the consumption of non-renewable resources
- Efficient use of energy, materials and natural capital
- Replacing non-renewable with renewable resources
- Creating an energy supply based on renewable energies.

A circular economy builds on self-responsibility of economic actors and higher competitiveness through more efficient free market solutions, technical and commercial innovation, whereas a green economy builds on corporate social responsibility (CSR), neglecting the regional job creation potential of a low-carbon resource-efficient economy.

External factors will increase the competitiveness of a circular economy. Rising resource prices mean:
- Today's goods in the market are the resources of tomorrow at yesterday's resource prices – if ownership is retained by the manufacturers/fleet managers of goods.
- Retained ownership of goods includes materials and embodied energy/water, can best be achieved by selling goods as services in a performance economy.
- Selling performance implies an internalisation of the costs of risk and waste, giving economic incentives for loss prevention and waste prevention over the full lifetime of products, leading to cost reductions and increased competitiveness.
- Selling performance instead of goods is the most profitable form of a circular economy.

Sustainable framework conditions:
- Do not tax renewable resources including human labour, a simple and convincing principle, compared to, for example, an ecological-social market economy
- Do not levy value-added tax (VAT) on value conservation activities
- Give carbon credits to carbon emission prevention (stock) at the same rate as carbon emission reductions (flow).

Introduction
"Previous patterns of growth have brought increased prosperity, but through intensive and often inefficient use of resources. The role of biodiversity, ecosystems and their services is largely undervalued, the costs of waste are often not reflected in prices, current markets and public policies cannot fully deal with competing demands on strategic resources such as minerals, land, water and biomass. This calls for a coherent and integrated response over a wide range of policies in order to deal with expected resource constraints and to sustain our prosperity in the long run." (EU COM(2011) 571 final)

This statement by the European Commission analyses today's resource efficiency and policy shortcomings. But it does not give solutions, it does not address labour as a resource and it leaves out a number of other challenges.

Economic actors in the circular economy have started to tackle many of these issues in a bottom-up approach by introducing new private sector business models of the circular economy, such as 'reuse, repair and remanufacture instead of replace', and 'selling goods as services'.

This includes an efficient use of labour as a renewable resource with a qualitative edge and "an economy as if people mattered" (Schumacher, 1973).

The multiple advantages of a circular economy were described decades ago by Stahel and Reday (1976/1981), and have started to transcend into policy making, as for instance in the 2008 EU waste directive. However, politicians' reflexes are still geared to overcome economic problems by promoting growth in the industrial production economy – witness the 'cash for clunkers' initiatives in 22 countries in 2010 – or by focussing on singular issues, such as environmental solutions. The quest for sustainable (holistic) solutions, which would simultaneously address economic, social and environmental issues, is jeopardised by the 'silo' structures of public administrations, academia and many corporations. Stahel (2001) showed that most sustainable solutions are intersectoral and interdisciplinary and thus contradict existing regulations, do not fit into academic career structures and demand a 'new think'.

This chapter shows the advantages inherent in the circular economy and argues that the shift to a circular economy can be accelerated by one simple shift in public policy – adapting the tax system to the principles of sustainability by not taxing renewable resources, including work. This will bring about a rapid expansion not only of the circular economy for manufactured capital (infrastructure, equipment and goods) but equally of all other economic activities based on stock optimisation and 'caring', such as health services, education, organic agriculture, producing goods from such locally available renewable materials as leather, wood and wool. Caring is also the foundation for maintaining our cultural heritage.

A circular economy is about economics and profit maximisation

This section details the circular economy, its focus on stock optimisation, and its structure of three loops of different nature and five principles. It explains why reuse and service-life extension of goods are the most profitable and resource efficient business models of the circular economy. From an economics view, maintaining value and performance of stock replaces value added of flow, and utilisation value replaces exchange value as the central notion of economic value.

Before 2012, few studies existed which analysed the economic benefits of a circular economy on a national or supranational level. In time for the World Economic Forum 2012 in Davos, the UK-based Ellen MacArthur Foundation (2012) published a report which calculates that a circular economy (better design and more efficient use of material) could save European manufacturers USD 630 billion a year by 2025. The report produced by consultancy McKinsey, only covers five sectors that represent a little less than half of the GDP contribution of EU manufacturing, but still calculates that greater resource efficiency could deliver multi-billion euro savings equivalent to 23% of current spending on manufacturing inputs.

The following abstract of *The Product-Life Factor* (Stahel, 1982) for the Mitchell Prize Competition 1982 on 'The role of the private sector in a sustainable society' is still an excellent summary of the circular economy:

"The extension of the use-life of goods is, first, a sensible point at which to start a gradual transition towards a sustainable society in which progress is made consistent with the world's finite resource base and, second, a strategy consistent with an active and independent role for the private sector. Product-life, or the period over which products and goods are used, governs their replacement speed and thus the consumption of natural resources required for their manufacture and the amount of waste they create. Shortening product-life increases demand for replacement goods where these can be afforded. Extending product-life optimises the total life-span of goods and reduces depletion of natural resources and consequently waste; it builds on and increases wealth. Compared to fast-replacement, product-life extension is a substitution of service activities for extractive and manufacturing industries, and a replacement of large-scale capital-intensive companies by smaller, labour-intensive, locally integrated work units. The private sector, whether R&D, manufacturing or finance, will find innumerable business opportunities in product-life extension activities – reuse, repair, reconditioning and recycling. Indeed, while increasing the number of skilled jobs available and reducing our dependence on strategic materials, such activities will provide the private sector with fresh impetus to make cheaper goods available as part of a self-replenishing economy built on a closed-loop pattern which allows a substitution of manpower for energy. In this way, unemployment and poverty which certainly aggravate the fundamental instability of the world economy might be substantially reduced. The private sector has, moreover, resources and skills that uniquely qualify it to initiate this transition towards a sustainable society where a balanced use of resources and other societal goals are achieved. Potential disincentives and obstacles can, we believe, be overcome with appropriate education and fiscal and policy measures." (Stahel, 1982)

A circular economy is about stock optimisation. New metrics to measure changes in the quantity and quality of stock – wealth in the form of manufactured capital stock, but also of health, education and skills – are needed to manage stock. We know how much money governments spend on building schools and employing teachers, but we do not know if students are better prepared for life, as a result. The stock of buildings in a given country and their qualitative conditions (thermal insulation, annual energy consumption) are not known, nor the residual service-life of infrastructure or technical equipment – which makes a national stock and thus wealth management difficult.

Turning the linear industrial economy into a loop or circular economy is, by definition, reducing the economic importance of resource extraction and waste management, and also reducing the environmental impairment caused by these industrial sectors. This change of focus from a linear throughput to a stock management opens opportunities in three loops of different characteristics, which are described in this section: (a) a reuse and remarketing loop for goods, (b) a loop of product-life extension activities of goods, and (c) a recycling loop for molecules (secondary resources).

A circular economy is about material and resource sufficiency and efficiency
This section presents new metrics to measure material efficiency, and quantifies the reductions in material consumption and emissions that can be achieved in the circular economy.

Stahel (1985) showed that many different types of innovation to increase material efficiency exist in the circular economy, including technical, commercial and 'utilisation' innovation. Technical innovation includes systems solution instead of product innovation (e.g., Plane Transport Systems).

A longer utilisation – long life products, reuse and service-life extension of goods and components – are one option. A more intensive use of goods is another utilisation innovation to achieve a higher material efficiency, for instance through shared utilisation (together: public transport) or serial utilisation of goods (one after another: washing machines in Laundromats and rental cars). These options need a 'new relationship with goods' and have extensively been discussed in the early 1990s (IFG, 1993) but are only now finding a real interest on both the supply and demand side, for example in car sharing initiatives.

Two distinctively different types of resource efficiency govern the circular economy: loop 1 in Figure 1 is about resource sufficiency in the reuse and service-life extension of manufactured capital, loop 2 is about material efficiency in recycling materials (molecules).

The strategies of loop 1 are product specific – re-refining engine oil, solvents and other products with a catalytic function need a different approach from the service-life extension activities for buildings or mobile durable goods. The latter's resource efficiency can be improved by modular system design, component standardisation and other eco-design (design for environment) approaches which are now known and well documented.

The strategies of loop 2 are material specific – metals, ceramic materials and plastic use processes of physical and chemical recycling often derived from manufacturing processes, as well as new processes such as the depolymerisation of polymers. Materials with a low price/weight ratio, such as brick and concrete waste from demolishing buildings, are best crushed, using mobile equipment, for reuse as recycling concrete on-site for new constructions.

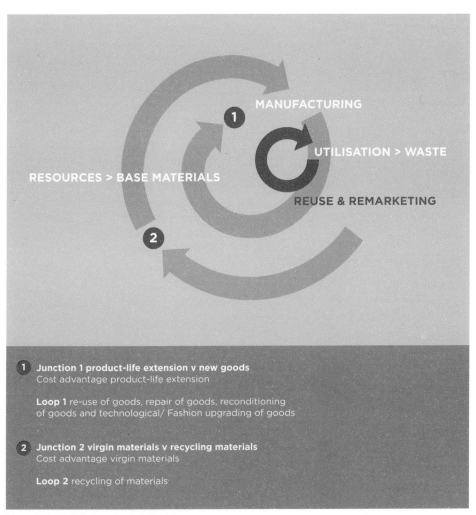

Figure 1 **The main loops of a circular economy**
Source: Stahel W R and Reday G (1976/1981)

All materials come with a multiple backpack *(rucksack)* of mining waste (Schmidt-Bleek, 1993) and environmental impairment. These backpacks differ for each material and are highest for rare metals such as gold (with a backpack of 500,000), lowest for plastics (with a backpack of 0.1). Manufactured capital in the form of infrastructure, buildings, goods and components has individual accumulated backpacks of all the materials and energies they embed, which have to be calculated individually.

Manufactured capital contains, in addition to the backpacks of the materials it is made of, the sum of the embodied energy and GHG emissions as well as the (virtual) water of the manufacturing steps from basic materials into finished goods and up to the point of sale.

The reuse, remarketing and service-life extension activities in a circular economy preserve the mining backpacks of water and energy inputs and related GHG emissions in the manufacturing chain up to the point of sale, which are embodied in the finished goods. In addition, they also prevent the environmental impairment of the material recycling and/or waste management processes.

Higher resource efficiency also means reduced costs for material and energy procurement, as well as for waste disposal, waste water treatment and emissions.

**A circular economy is about an intelligent use of human labour –
job creation in a regional economy**
This section explains why human labour – work – is different from the other renewable resources: creative, versatile and adaptable, able to be educated but perishable if unused. The circular economy needs workers familiar with past technologies and thus offers jobs for 'silver workers'.

"Roughly three-quarters of all industrial energy consumption is associated with the extraction or production of basic materials like steel and cement, while only about one-quarter is used in the transformation of raw material into finished goods such as machines and buildings. The converse is true of labour, about three times as much being used in the conversion of materials to finished products as is required in the production of material." (Stahel & Reday-Mulvey, 1976 and 1981)

Compared to the traditional manufacturing process, the labour input of the circular economy is higher as (a) its economies of scale are limited in geographic and volume terms, and (b) remanufacturing comprises additional steps of dismantling, cleaning and quality control, which are absent in manufacturing.

No estimations exist yet on the impact of a circular economy on a national labour market. Yet, employment is at the heart of the social pillar of sustainability.

Furthermore, substituting labour for other resources is also an intelligent solution for reasons which are inherent in human labour – it is the only renewable resource with a qualitative characteristic. Work is the most versatile and adaptable of all resources, with a strong but perishable qualitative edge: (a) It is the only resource capable of creativity and with the capacity to produce innovative solutions, and (b) human skills deteriorate if unused – continuity of work and continued learning are necessary to maintain skills and upgrade capabilities. A person who has been unemployed for a few years risks becoming unemployable.

Governments should give priority to human labour in resource use because a barrel of oil or a ton of coal left in the ground for another decade will not deteriorate, nor will it demand social welfare, and not taxing labour reduces incentives for illegal labour in the shadow economy and thus reduces the costs for governments to monitor and punish abuses.

A circular economy is about caring

One of the objectives of a circular economy is to preserve the quality, performance and value of the existing stock, wealth and welfare. This certainly concerns manufactured capital, such as buildings, infrastructure, equipment and goods and is a key criteria if selling performance (goods as services).

Stock management needs statistics and metrics to measure the variations of wealth due to variations in the quality of stock. GDP is a flow metric, ignoring if our wealth – the stock – has increased as a result of the flow. This situation has been compared to a bath tub where only the inflow of hot and cold water is measured, but the outflow and the water level are ignored (Giarini & Stahel, 1989).

And stock management includes people's skills, education and health, knowledge and know-how. Preserving culture is also linked to stock, not flow management; maintaining UNESCO world heritage sites, museums and examples of technological achievements will all profit from the shift in taxation towards the non-taxation of renewable resources. And caring is a high-quality world: Stradivari instruments and expensive watches do not live forever by design, but through periodic remanufacturing, motivated by caring.

Caring is a key characteristics of managing stock – caring for keeping up existing values and qualities. Most car owners will credit the manufacturer of their vehicle for its continued reliable functioning, rather than their mechanic who provides the maintenance and repair services. A change in popular values and beliefs would multiply the perception of caring as a pillar of the (circular) economy. The fleet of vintage and old-timer cars in the UK could be a point in case.

Retained ownership of goods and embodied material provides future resource security
This section looks at why selling goods as service, or performance, is the most profitable and resource efficient business model of the circular economy. By focusing on systems solutions, it internalises the cost of risk and of waste; by retaining the ownership of goods and the embodied resources, it creates a corporate and national resource security for the future.

Many economists have a problem accepting that this is a discontinuity in traditional economic business models, and look at the sale of performance as an extension of the aftermarket (Cohen, M.A. et al, 2006).

Economic actors retaining material ownership over the full life of their products gain a future resource security but accept a liability for the performance of their goods. Such a performance economy (Stahel, 2010) is based on the triple objectives of more growth and more jobs in combination with substantially reduced resource consumption. This triple objective can be achieved through three new business models: producing performance, selling performance and maintaining performance over time.

Success is measured using two new metrics in the form of absolute decoupling indicators: value per weight ($/kg) and labour-input per weight (man-hours/kg).

In the performance economy, providing materials services can be achieved, for instance, by building residential housing without capital. The developer rents all material and equipment from the manufacturers, say over a period of 50 years, who in return receive a yearly rent, financed by the rental income from the apartments. As the manufacturers have to give a 50 year guarantee for their material, they will make sure that the most appropriate material is used and applied correctly (renewable urban space initiative, in: Stahel, 2010, p156).

Selling performance differs according to the characteristics of products and is widely present in today's economy: selling goods as services by operating private and public networks (railways, telecom, motorways, airports); chemical management services and rent-a-molecule; energy management and integrated crop management services; rental and operational leasing of real estate; selling custom-made indoor climate for energy companies; private finance initiatives (known as PFIs) as a strategy to sell the utilisation of infrastructure according to the 'consumer pays principle', such as the French and Italian toll motorways; facility management of real estate and industrial plants; textile leasing (professional attire, hotel and hospital linen). These are but a few examples of the business model of selling performance, which also include rent-a-wash, rent-a-molecule and chemical leasing, as well as renting fashionable consumer goods (taking the waste out of fashion, see websites to rent ladies' handbags).

Selling performance is the most profitable and most material-efficient business model of the circular economy, as it is built on exploiting the small loops. It focuses on utilisation optimisation and exploits resource efficiency as well as sufficiency and prevention options to gain financial advantages and higher competitiveness. And it can be applied to all types of goods, (see Table 1, Key business strategies of the functional service economy).

Water and energy savings, as well as waste prevention, now become profitable activities that positively impact the financial bottom line of corporations. Whereas in the industrial economy, sufficiency and prevention options during the utilisation phase of goods present a loss of income, and are thus undesirable.

Selling performance, results, utilisation, services instead of goods means that economic actors:
a) retain the ownership of goods and embodied resources; and,
b) internalise the cost of risk and of waste.
By comparison, the industrial economy maximises its profit by externalising the cost of risk and of waste. After the point of sale, it offers a warranty for a limited period of time and limited to manufacturing defects.

By internalising the cost of risk and the cost of waste, economic actors selling performance have an economic incentive to prevent any future liability after the point of sale.

Retaining ownership of their goods and embodied resources over the full life of their products gives corporations in times of rising resource prices (see next section) a high future resource security and resource price guarantee as well as a competitive cost advantage against throughput-based competitors, along the lines of:

"The goods of today are the resources of tomorrow at yesterday's prices"

Table 1 **Key business strategies of the functional service economy**

Corporate strategies	S1 Prevention strategies	S2 Manufacturers selling performance, services or results	S3 Manufacturers Fleet managers with loop responsibility	S4 Fleet managers with maintenance & operation responsibility	R Independent remanufacturers
and product groups					
	SCIENCE				
Consumption goods (fuel)					
Dissipative goods (paint)					
Catalytic goods (engine oil, solvents)					
Durable mobile goods (cars)					
Durable immobile goods (buildings)					

Rotated labels within matrix: Knowledge-based solutions · Vertical integration · EPeR Extended Performance Responsibility · An economy in closed loops · Utilisation optimisation · Product-life extension · JOBS Job creation potential

Source: Stahel, W.R. (2010) The Performance Economy, p102.

Buying performance is the demand side strategy equivalent to selling performance. Buying goods as services creates the same resource efficiency advantages and can be regarded as a new green public procurement policy. Buying services instead of hardware is the preferred procurement option of parts of the US administration, such as NASA and the Pentagon, and has sparked a number of innovative start-up companies. NASA now buys exclusively orbital services from companies such as Space-X; the space shuttle was the last NASA-owned and operated hardware to provide Earth orbit services.

Michelin provides tyre-use services to all parts of the US armed forces: for aircraft tyres, a fee per landing is charged; vehicle tyres pay a fixed fee per 100 miles. This service of 'pay by the mile' is now also offered to French and US fleet managers of lorries, using a business model of mobile tyre service workshops to make tyres last as long as safely possible.

Policy for material efficiency: the role of sustainable taxation and sustainable framework conditions
Sustainable framework conditions should treat the circular economy on its own merits, by:

a) Not taxing work – human – labour as a zero-carbon renewable resource.
b) Not charging VAT on such value preservation activities as reuse, repair and remanufacturing, with the possible exception of technologic upgrading activities. Major re-marketing activities, such as flea-markets and ebay, are already de facto exempt from VAT.
c) Giving carbon credits for the prevention of GHG emissions, not only for their reduction. The small loops (Figure 1) constitute a prevention of GHG emissions (and waste) but receive no carbon credits under any of the existing or planned GHG emission programmes, such as the Kyoto Protocol, which are based on the linear thinking of the industrial economy: first pollute, then reduce pollution to receive carbon credits.

Sustainable politics should build on simple and convincing principles, such as: Do not tax what you want to foster, punish unwanted effects instead. Also, it should promote sustainable solutions. Ideally, sustainable solutions create self-reinforcing virtuous circles, which guarantee their longevity.

Not taxing renewable resources, including work, and taxing non-renewable ones instead, creates virtuous self-reinforcing circles, by creating incentives to work more (no penalty for higher income) and by creating more wealth from less new resource input (increasing caring in resource use, including long-term resource ownership).

Sustainable taxation should reward desired developments and discourage unwanted effects of activities. In a sustainable economy, taxes on renewable resources, including work – human labour – are counterproductive and should be abandoned. The resulting loss of state revenue could be compensated by taxing the consumption of non-renewable resources in the form of materials and energies, and of undesired wastes and emissions. Such a shift in taxation would promote and reward a circular economy with its local low-carbon and low-resource solutions. These are inherently more labour-intensive than manufacturing because economies of scale in a circular economy are limited. Taxes on non-renewable resources could be charged in a similar way to today's VAT, also for imported goods.

The intelligent use of human labour has traditionally been discouraged through taxation, whereas the waste of it has been 'encouraged' in some industrialised countries through generous welfare. This shows that the role of work as a renewable resource in the economy has been misunderstood by policymakers.

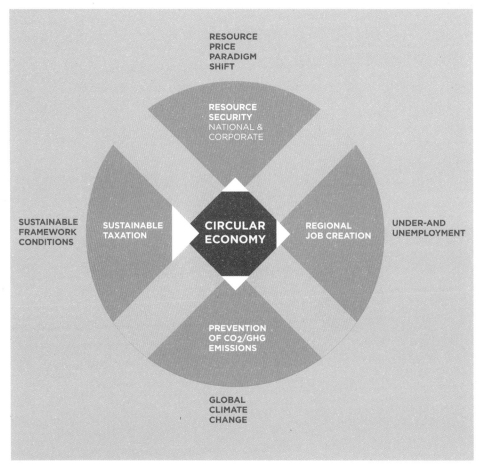

Figure 2 **Sustainable taxation will promote the circular economy which in turn boosts resource security, regional job creation and the prevention of GHG emission** (Stahel, 2011)

Summary

The linear industrial economy is best in overcoming situations of scarcity of food, goods, shelter. But in a situation of saturated markets, a circular economy is best suited to manage existing stock. In 1980, the market penetration for durable household goods in France was already above 90% for all social classes (Stahel & Jackson, 1993). In Germany, from 1995 onwards, the number of cars scrapped each year has been roughly the same as the number of cars newly registered. Continued production in saturated markets constitutes a substitution of, not an addition to, wealth, at the cost of "intensive and often inefficient use of resources" (EU COM(2011) 571 final).

For the last 100 years, resource prices for energy and material have constantly decreased; maintaining ownership of materials to assure access to future resources made little sense. At the beginning of the 21st century, this trend has changed, and it is expected that resource prices in the 21st century will constantly increase – a theory formulated by experts at the European Commission and prominently by the asset manager Jeremy Grantham in 2011 who called it "the big paradigm shift". Resource security could, therefore, become a major political bone of contention; and economic actors maintaining resource ownership will enjoy a certain guarantee of resource availability and price in the future, at the same time providing resource security for nations.

A sustainable tax policy of not taxing renewable resources, including work, constitutes a very powerful lever to accelerate, boost and generalise the circular economy. Its positive impacts on resource security and regional job creation, while simultaneously reducing GHG emissions, are summarised in Figure 2.

References
Allwood, J.M., Ashby, M.F., Gutowski, T.G., Worrell, E. (2011) Material efficiency: a white paper; in. *Resources, Conservation and Recycling 55* (2011) p362-381. Elsevier

Cohen, M.A., Agrawal N. and Agrawal V. (2006) Winning in the Aftermarket; in: *Harvard Business Review,* May 2006, p129-138

Ellen MacArthur Foundation (ed.) (2012) Towards the Circular Economy, economic and business rationale for an accelerated transition

European Commission (2011) Roadmap to a Resource Efficient Europe, SEC(2011) 1067 final; COM(2011) 571 final. Brussels

European Directive 2008/98/EC of the European Parliament and of the Council of 19 November 2008 on waste and repealing certain Directives. Brussels

Giarini, O. and Stahel, W.R. (1989) *The Limits to Certainty,* facing risks in the new service economy; Kluwer Academic Publishers, Dordrecht (1st edition)

Granthams, J. (2011) *http://dailyartifacts.com/summary-of-jeremy-granthams-letter*

Harvard Business School (1994), *Xerox: Design for Environment,* case study N9-794-022, HBS Boston, MA

Jackson, T. (2009) Prosperity without growth, economics for a finite planet

Orr, S.G. (ed.) (1982) *An Inquiry into the Nature of Sustainable Societies: The Role of the Private Sector, the 1982 Mitchell Prizes,* Houston Area Research Center, The Woodlands, TX

Schmidt-Bleek, F. (1993) *Wieviel Umwelt braucht der Mensch? MIPS – das Mass für ökologisches Wirtschaften.* Birkhäuser Berlin. (Material Input Per unit of Service (MIPS) – the metric for an ecologic economy)

Schumacher, E.F. (1973) *Small is beautiful, economics as if people mattered,* Harper and Row, Publishers. Chapter 1: The Greatest Resource – Education

Smith, V.M., Keolian, G.A. (2004) The value of remanufactured engines, life-cycle environmental and economic perspectives, *Journal of Industrial Ecology,* 8(1-2) p193-222

Sinn, H.W., (2008) *Das grüne Paradoxon: Warum man das Angebot bei der Klimapolitik nicht vergessen darf,* Perspektiven der Wirtschaftspolitik 9, München, p109-142

Söderholm, P. (2011) Taxing virgin natural resources: Lessons from aggregates taxation in Europe. *Resources, Conservation and Recycling.* 55: p911-922

Stahel, W. R., Jackson, T. (1993) Optimal utilisation and durability – towards a new definition of the service economy; in: Jackson, Tim (ed.) *Clean Production Strategies, developing preventive environmental management in the industrial economy,* Lewis Publishers, Boca Raton, p261-291

Stahel, W.R. and Reday, G. (1976) *The potential for substituting manpower for energy,* report to the Commission of the European Communities, Brussels

Stahel, W.R. and Reday, G. (1981) *Jobs for Tomorrow, the potential for substituting manpower for energy,* Vantage Press, New York, N.Y.

Stahel, W. R., (1982) The Product-Life Factor; available at http://www.product-life.org/en/major-publications/the-product-life-factor

Stahel, W. R. (1985) Hidden innovation: R&D in a sustainable society, in *Science & Public Policy,* journal of the international Science Policy Foundation, 13(4) Special Issue: The Hidden Wealth

Stahel, W. R., (1997) The functional economy: cultural and organizational change; in: Richards, Deanna J., *The industrial green game,* National Academy Press, Washington DC. p91-100

Stahel, W. R. (2001) *Studie über die kulturellen Faktoren der Wettbewerbsfähigkeit von nach-haltigen Lösungsansätzen* in der Praxis; BMVIT, Wien und Land Steiermark, Graz (research report). (Study on the cultural factors of the competitiveness of sustainable solution approaches in practice)

Stahel, W. R. (2010) *The Performance Economy,* 2nd edition, Palgrave Macmillan, Basingstoke

WRAP (2009) *Meeting the UK climate change challenge: the contribution of resource efficiency,* project code EVA 128, November 2009. London

A FAREWELL TO FOSSIL FUELS
ANSWERING THE ENERGY CHALLENGE*

Amory B Lovins

With the costs of oil and coal rising, the United States and other countries need to wean themselves off fossil fuels, a goal best accomplished by making buildings and vehicles more efficient and switching to renewable power. The task might seem quixotic, but it actually will not require miracles - just the widespread application of existing technology. This transition could be led by business for profit. In the United States, the process could be sped up by revenue-neutral policies enacted by US states or federal agencies, and it would need from Congress no new taxes, subsidies, mandates, or laws.

Amory B Lovins is Chair and Chief Scientist of Rocky Mountain Institute and the senior author of *Reinventing Fire: Bold Business Solutions for the New Energy Era.*

ert@rmi.org

Rocky Mountain Institute
www.rmi.org

*This article was first published in Foreign Affairs Volume 91, March/April 2012. Reproduced with kind permission of Foreign Affairs.

Nearly 90% of the world's economy is fuelled every year by digging up and burning about four cubic miles of the rotted remains of primeval swamp goo. With extraordinary skill, the world's most powerful industries have turned that oil, gas, and coal into affordable and convenient fuels and electricity that have created wealth, helped build modern civilisation, and enriched the lives of billions.

Yet, today, the rising costs and risks of these fossil fuels are undercutting the security and prosperity they have enabled. Each day, the United States spends about USD 2 billion buying oil and loses another USD 4 billion indirectly to the macroeconomic costs of oil dependence, the microeconomic costs of oil price volatility, and the cost of keeping military forces ready for intervention in the Persian Gulf.

In all, the United States spends one-sixth of its GDP on oil, not counting any damage to foreign policy, global stability, public health, and the environment. The hidden costs are also massive for coal and are significant for natural gas, too. Even if oil and coal prices were not high, volatile, and rising, risks such as fuel insecurity and dependence, pollution-caused illnesses, energy-driven conflicts over water and food, climate change, and geopolitical tensions would make oil and coal unattractive.

Weaning the United States from those fossil fuels would require two big shifts: in oil and electricity. These are distinct – nearly half of electricity is made from coal, and almost none is made from oil – but power plants and oil burning each account for over two-fifths of the carbon that is emitted by fossil-fuel use. In the United States, three-fourths of electricity powers buildings, three-fourths of oil fuels transportation, and the remaining oil and electricity run factories. So saving oil and electricity is chiefly about making buildings, vehicles, and factories far more efficient – no small task.

But epochal energy shifts have happened before. In 1850, most US homes used whale-oil lamps, and whaling was the country's fifth-biggest industry. But as whale populations dwindled, the price of whale oil rose, so between 1850 and 1859, coal-derived synthetic fuels grabbed more than five-sixths of the lighting market. In 1859, Edwin Drake struck oil, and kerosene, thanks to generous tax breaks, soon took over. Whalers, astounded that they had run out of customers before they had run out of whales, begged for federal subsidies on national security grounds, but Thomas Edison's 1879 invention of electric lighting snuffed out their industry. Whales had been accidentally saved by technological innovators and profit-maximising capitalists.

As the world shuddered from the 1973 oil shock, the economist Phil Gramm predicted that just as with whale oil, innovators would innovate, capitalists would invest, markets would clear, and substitutes for petroleum would ultimately emerge. He was right. By 2010, the United States was using 60% less oil to make USD 1 of GDP than it had in 1975. Now, the other shoe is dropping: since its use in the United States peaked in 2005, coal has lost one-fourth of its share of the US electric services market to renewable energy, natural gas, and efficient use. After just a few centuries, the anomalous era of oil and coal is gradually starting to come to an end. In its place, the era of everlasting energy is dawning.

Underlying this shift in supply is the inexorable shrinkage in the energy needed to create USD 1 of GDP. In 1976, I heretically suggested that this 'energy intensity' could fall by two-thirds by 2025. By 2010, it had fallen by half, driven by no central plan or visionary intent but only by the perennial quest for profit, security, and health. Still-newer methods, without further inventions, could reduce US energy intensity by another two-thirds over the next four decades, with huge economic benefits. In fact, as *Reinventing Fire*, the new book from my organisation, Rocky Mountain Institute (RMI), details, a US economy that has grown by 158% by 2050 could need no oil, no coal, no nuclear energy, and one-third less natural gas – and cost USD 5 trillion less than business as usual, ignoring all hidden costs. Today's fossil carbon emissions could also fall by more than four-fifths without even putting a price on them.

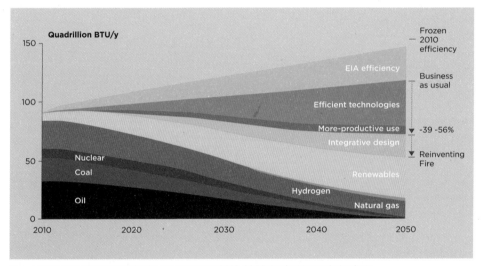

Figure 1 **Energy consumption in the US economy 2010-2050** *Rocky Mountain Institute*

By 2050, the US can phase out its use of oil, coal, and nuclear energy by using energy more efficiently and relying on natural gas and renewables to fuel the US economy. The energy efficiency opportunity accounts for more than half of the business-as-usual consumption in 2050 (assuming frozen efficiency from 2010–50). Aggressively exploiting this opportunity makes the transition from oil and coal cost-effective, and enables a roughly one-third reduction in natural gas consumption and a major investment in renewable energy. Note that if the hydrogen shown were all reformed from natural gas, it would come half from gas and half from steam.

Rocky Mountain Institute © 2011. Published by Chelsea Green in Reinventing Fire.
For more information see www.RMI.org/ReinventingFire.

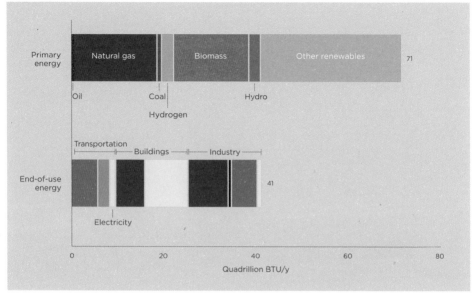

Figure 2 **Reinventing Fire: US energy consumption 2050** *Rocky Mountain Institute*

Reinventing Fire describes an energy future markedly different from business-as-usual official forecasts. For the same level of economic activity (2050 GDP 2.58 times 2010's), *Reinventing Fire* envisions an economy that uses 71 quadrillion BTUs of primary energy in 2050, 39% less than the business-as-usual forecast or 21% below 2010's level. *Reinventing Fire* shows how the primary energy needed can come from roughly one-fourth natural gas (the same share as now), and the rest from renewables rather than, as now, from oil and coal. Wind, solar, biomass, and natural gas account for 98% of primary energy used in *Reinventing Fire* in 2050, the rest from coal and oil. If the hydrogen shown were all reformed from natural gas, it would come half from gas and half from steam.

This transformation requires pursuing three agendas. First, radical automotive efficiency can make electric propulsion affordable; heavy vehicles, too, can save most of their fuel; and all vehicles can be used more productively. Second, new designs can make buildings and factories several times as efficient as they are now. Third, modernising the electric system to make it diverse, distributed, and renewable can also make it clean, reliable, and secure. These ambitious shifts may seem quixotic, but sometimes tough problems are best solved by enlarging their boundaries, as General Dwight Eisenhower reputedly advised.

Thus, it is easier to solve the problems of all four energy-using sectors – transportation, buildings, industry, and electricity – together than separately. For example, electric vehicles could recharge from or supply power to the electricity grid at times that compensate for variations in the output from wind and solar power. Synergies likewise arise from integrating innovations in technology, policy, design, and strategy, not just the first one or two.

This transition will require no technological miracles or social engineering – only the systematic application of many available, straightforward techniques. It could be led by business for profit and sped up by revenue-neutral policies enacted by US states or federal agencies, and it would need from Congress no new taxes, subsidies, mandates, or laws. The United States' most effective institutions – the private sector, civil society, and the military – could bypass its least effective institutions. At last, Americans could make energy do their work without working their undoing.

Mobility without oil
The United States burns one-fourth of the world's oil, half in automobiles (which comprise cars and light trucks). Two-thirds of cars' fuel use is caused by their weight, yet for the past quarter century, US cars have gained weight twice as fast as their drivers. Now, lighter metals and synthetic materials are reversing automotive obesity. Ultralight, ultrastrong carbon-fibre composites can trigger dramatic weight savings, improve safety, and offset the carbon fibre's higher cost with simpler automaking (needing four-fifths less capital) and smaller powertrains. In 2011, lightweighting became the auto industry's hottest trend. Ford's strategy rests on it, and the United States could lead it. So far, however, Germany has taken the lead: Volkswagen, BMW, and Audi all plan to be mass-producing carbon-fibre electric cars by 2013.

Ultralight, aerodynamic autos make electric propulsion affordable because they need fewer costly batteries or fuel cells. Rather than wringing pennies from old steel-stamping and engine technologies, automakers could exploit mutually reinforcing advances in carbon fibre, its structural manufacturing, and electric propulsion – a transition as game changing as the shift from typewriters to computers. BMW, whose chief executive has said, "We do not intend to be a typewriter maker," has confirmed that its planned 2013 electric car will pay for its carbon fibre by needing fewer batteries.

Electric autos are already far cheaper to fuel than gasoline autos, and they could also cost about the same to buy within a few decades. Until then, 'feebates' – rebates for more efficient new autos, paid for by equivalent fees on inefficient ones – could prevent sticker shock. In just two years, France, with the biggest of Europe's five feebate programmes, saw its new autos get more efficient three times as fast as before.

Well-designed US feebates, which could be enacted at the state level, need not cost the government a penny. They could expand customers' choices and boost automakers' and dealers' profit margins.

Autos could also be used more productively. If the government employed new methods to charge drivers for road infrastructure by the mile, its insolvent Highway Trust Fund would not need to rely on taxing dwindling gallons of fuel. Information technologies could smooth traffic flow, enhance public transit, and promote vehicle- and ridesharing. Better-designed layouts of communities could increase affordability, liveability, and developers' profits. Together, these proven innovations could get Americans to their destinations with half the driving (or less) and USD 0.4 trillion less cost. RMI's analysis found that by 2050, the United States could deliver far greater mobility by making vehicles efficient, productive, and oil-free. Autos powered by any mix of electricity, hydrogen fuel cells, and advanced biofuels could get the equivalent of 125 to 240 miles per gallon of gasoline and save trillions of dollars. By 2050, 'drilling under Detroit' could profitably displace nearly 15 million barrels of oil per day – 1.5 times as much as Saudi Arabia's current daily output.

Heavy vehicles present similar opportunities. From 2005 to 2010, Walmart saved 60% of its heavy-truck fleet's fuel through smarter designs and changes in driver behaviour and logistics. Aeronautical engineers are designing aeroplanes that will be three to five times as efficient as today's. Super-efficient trucks and aeroplanes could use advanced biofuels or hydrogen, or trucks could burn natural gas, but no vehicles would need oil. Advanced biofuels, two-thirds made from waste, would require no cropland, protecting soil and the climate. The US military's ongoing advances in efficiency will speed all these innovations in the civilian sector, which uses more than 50 times as much oil, just as military research and development created the internet, GPS, and the microchip and jet-engine industries.

US gasoline demand peaked in 2007; the oil use of the countries of the Organization for Economic Cooperation and Development peaked in 2005. With China and India pursuing efficient and electric vehicles, Deutsche Bank forecasts in 2009 that world oil use could begin to decline after 2016. In fact, the world is nearing 'peak oil' – not in supply but in demand. Oil is simply becoming uncompetitive even at low prices before it becomes unavailable even at high prices.

Saving electricity
The next big shift is to raise electricity productivity faster than the economy grows – starting with the United States' 120 million buildings. Even though US buildings are projected to provide 70% more total floor space in 2050, they could use far less energy. Investing an extra USD 0.5 trillion on existing or emerging energy-efficiency technologies and better-integrated designs could save building owners USD 1.9 trillion by tripling or quadrupling energy productivity. These straightforward improvements range from installing insulation, weather-stripping, and caulking to using more efficient equipment and controls, adopting better lighting design, and simply making new buildings the right shape and facing them in the right direction.

An even more powerful innovation, called 'integrative design', can often save far more energy still, yet at lower cost. Integrative design optimises a whole building, factory, vehicle, or device for multiple benefits, not isolated components for single benefits. For example, in 2010, the Empire State Building remanufactured its 6,514 windows onsite into 'superwindows', which pass light but block heat. Requiring a third less air conditioning on hot days saved USD 17 million of the project's capital cost immediately, partly funding this and other improvements. In just three years, energy savings above 40% will repay the owners' total energy-saving investment.

Integrative design's expanding returns are even more impressive when built in from scratch. From tropical to subarctic climates, new passively heated and cooled buildings can replace furnaces and air conditioners with super-insulation, heat recovery, and design that exploits the local climate. European companies have built 32,000 such structures at roughly normal capital cost and cost-effectively retrofitted similar performance into Swedish apartments constructed in the 1950s and into century-old Viennese apartments. The business case would be even stronger if it included the valuable indirect benefits of these more comfortable, pleasant, and healthful buildings: higher office labour productivity and retail sales, faster learning in classrooms, faster healing in hospitals, and higher real estate values everywhere. Integrative design can also help double industrial energy productivity, saving USD 0.5 trillion. Pumps, for example, are the world's biggest user of electric motors. Pumps, motors, and controls can improve, but first replacing long, thin, crooked pipes with short, fat, straight ones often avoids 80 to 90% of the usual friction, saving 10 times as much coal back at the power plant. When RMI and its industrial partners recently redesigned existing factories valued at more than USD 30 billion, our designs cut predicted energy use by about 30 to 60% with payback times of a few years. In new facilities, our designs were expected to save around 40 to 90% of energy use while usually reducing capital costs. This is not rocket science – just elegantly frugal whole-system thinking.

Adopting energy-saving innovations as quickly nationwide as some US states do today will require patiently fixing perverse incentives, sharing benefits between landlords and tenants, allocating capital wisely, and designing thoughtfully – not just copying the old drawings. None of this barrier busting is easy, but the rewards are great. Since the Dow Chemical Company embraced efficiency innovation in the 1990s, its USD 1 billion investment has returned USD 19 billion. Savings and returns, far from petering out, often kept rising as the engineers learned new tricks faster than they exhausted old ones.

Repowering prosperity

The United States must replace its aging, dirty, and insecure electric system by 2050 just to offset the loss of power plants that are being retired. Any replacement will cost about USD 6 trillion in net present value, whether it is more of the same, new nuclear power plants and 'clean coal', or centralised or distributed renewable sources. But these differ profoundly in the kinds of risks they involve – in terms of security, safety, finance, technology, fuel, water, climate, and health – and in how they affect innovation, entrepreneurship, and customer choice.

Choosing electricity sources is complicated by copious disinformation, such as the myth that nuclear power was thriving in the United States until environmentalists derailed it after the March 1979 Three Mile Island meltdown. In fact, bad economics made orders for nuclear power plants in the United States fall by 90% from 1973 to 1975 and dry up completely by 1978. Indeed, soaring capital costs eventually halted nuclear expansion in all market-based power systems, and by 2010, all 66 reactors under construction worldwide had been bought by central planners.

Even after the US government raised its subsidies for new reactors in 2005 to at least their construction costs, not one of the 34 proposed units could attract private capital; they simply had no business case. Neither do proposed 'small modular reactors': nuclear reactors do not scale down well, and the economies sought from mass-producing hypothetical small reactors cannot overcome the head start enjoyed by small modular renewables, which have attracted USD 1 trillion since 2004 and are adding another USD 0.25 trillion a year. After the 2011 Fukushima nuclear disaster, John Rowe, chair of Exelon (the United States' biggest nuclear power producer), pronounced the nuclear renaissance dead. In truth, market forces had killed it years earlier.

New coal and nuclear plants are so uneconomical that official US energy forecasts predict no new nuclear and few new coal projects will be launched. Investors are shunning their high costs and financial risks in favour of small, fast, modular renewable generators. These reduce the financial risk of building massive, slow, monolithic projects, and needing no fuel, they hedge against volatile gas prices. Already, wind and solar power's falling costs are beating fossil-fuelled power's and nuclear power's rising costs. Some solar panels now sell wholesale for less than USD 1 a watt (down 75% in three years), some installed solar-power systems in Germany sell for USD 2.80 a watt, and some US wind-power contracts charge less than three cents per kilowatt- hour – all far below recent forecasts. Solar power's plummeting cost, a stunning market success, is ruining some weaker or slower solar-cell-makers, but solar and wind power are extinguishing the prospects of coal and nuclear power around the world. So is cheap new natural gas – a valuable transitional resource if its many uncertainties can be resolved, but not a serious disappointment if they cannot, since higher efficiency and renewable energy should lower the demand for gas.

Skeptics of solar and wind power warn of their fluctuating output. But the grid can cope. Just as it routinely backs up nonworking coal-fired and nuclear plants with working ones, it can back up becalmed wind turbines or darkened solar cells with flexible generators (renewable or not) in other places or of other kinds, or with systems that voluntarily modulate demand. Even with little or no bulk power storage, diversified, forecastable, and integrated renewables can prove highly reliable. Such integration into a larger, more diverse grid is how in 2010 Denmark had the capacity to produce 36% of its electricity from renewables, including 26% from wind (in an average wind year), and how four German states were 43 to 52% wind-powered. But US and European studies have shown how whole continents could make 80% or more of their power renewably by operating existing assets differently within smarter grids, in markets that clear faster and serve larger areas.

Diverse, dispersed, renewable sources can also make the grid highly resilient. Centralised grids are vulnerable to cascading blackouts caused by natural disaster, accident, or malice. But grid reorganisations in Denmark and Cuba have shown how prolonged regional blackouts become impossible when distributed renewables, bypassing vulnerable power lines (where most failures start), feed local 'microgrids', which can stand alone if needed. The Pentagon, concerned about its own reliance on the commercial grid, shares this goal of resilience and this path to achieving it.

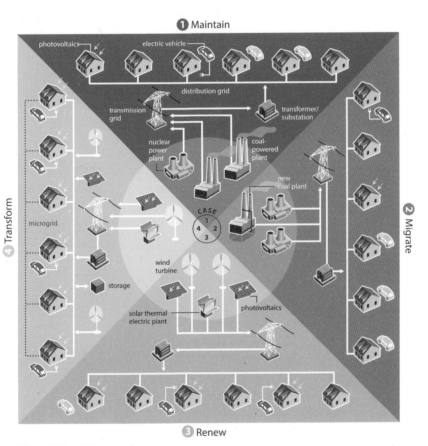

Figure 3 Electricity scenarios
Rocky Mountain Institute. Reproduced with kind permission of Chelsea Green

Reinventing Fire envisions a future electricity sector in which widespread energy efficiency adoption has flattened demand growth, demand response and energy storage technologies have enabled increased use of variable renewable generators, and environmental responsibility, fuel availability concerns, and competitive logic have increased distributed and grid-scale renewables to at least 80% of U.S. 2050 electricity generation. To assess the implications of this and other possible scenarios, RMI developed and analysed four patterns of how electricity might be generated, delivered, and consumed in the next 40 years. For these four cases – Maintain, Migrate, Renew, and Transform – RMI evaluated their performance in five areas: technical feasibility, affordability, reliability, environmental responsibility, and public acceptability. Full detail on the four cases at http://www.rmi.org/RFGraph-Electricity_scenarios

Individual households can also declare independence from power outages and utility bills, as mine has. In many parts of the United States, a private company can now install rooftop solar power with no money down and charge the customer less money per month to pay for it than the old electricity bill. These and other unregulated services could eventually create a 'virtual utility' that could largely or wholly bypass power companies, just as mobile phones bypassed landline phone companies – a prospect that worries utility executives but excites venture capitalists. Today, solar power is subsidised, although often less than fossil-fuelled or nuclear plants and their fuel. But sooner than those rivals could be built, solar power should win, even without subsidies.

In 2010, renewable sources, except for big hydropower dams, produced only 3% of the world's electricity, but for the third year running, they were responsible for nearly half of all new capacity. That same year, they won USD 151 billion of private investment and surpassed the total generating capacity of nuclear plants worldwide by adding more than 60 billion watts of capacity. The world can now manufacture that much new photovoltaic capacity every year, outpacing even wind power.

The United States is a leader in developing renewable technology but lags in installing it. In June 2010 alone, Germany, with less sun than Seattle, added 142% more solar-cell capacity than the United States did in all of 2010. Stop-and-go congressional policies sank US clean-energy investments from first place globally to third between 2008 and 2010. (Federal initiatives expiring in 2011-12 temporarily restored the US lead in 2011.) From 2005 to 2010, while the renewable fraction of the United States' electricity crawled from 9 to 10%, that of Portugal's soared from 17% to 45%. In 2010, congressional wrangling over the wind-power tax credit halved wind-power additions, while China doubled its wind capacity for the fifth year running and beat its 2020 target. The same year, 38% of China's net new capacity was renewable. China now leads the world in five renewable technologies and aims to in all.

Legacy industries erect many anticompetitive roadblocks to US renewable energy, often denying renewable power fair access to the grid or rejecting cheaper wind power to shield old plants from competition. In 34 US states, utilities earn more profit by selling more electricity and less if customers' bills fall. In 37 states, companies that reduce electricity demand are not allowed to bid in auctions for proposed new power supplies. But wherever such impediments are removed, efficiency and renewables win. In 2009, developers offered 4.4 billion watts of solar power cheaper than electricity from an efficient new gas-fired plant, so California's private utilities bought it – and in 2011, they were offered another 50 billion watts.

A cooler and safer world

This new energy future offers a pragmatic solution to climate change. Often assumed to be costly, reducing carbon emissions is actually profitable, since saving fuel costs less than buying fuel. Profits, jobs, and competitive advantage make for easier conversations than costs, burdens, and sacrifices, and they need no global treaties to drive them.

In 2009, the consulting firm McKinsey & Company found that projected greenhouse gas emissions could be cut by 70% by 2030 at a trivial average cost of USD 6 per metric ton of carbon dioxide equivalent (the standard unit of global-warming impact). Including newer technologies and integrative designs could save even more carbon more cheaply, and thus could more than meet the United States' obligations under the 1992 UN Framework Convention on Climate Change while saving USD 5 trillion.

Getting the United States off fossil fuels would transform its foreign policy. A world where the United States and other countries buy no oil because its price and price volatility exceed its value would have less oil-fed tyranny, corruption, terrorism, tension, and war. Washington, no longer needing an oil-centric foreign policy, could maintain normal relations with oil-exporting countries and treat diplomatic issues on their merits. The Pentagon would be pleased, too. Today, every one of the US military's nine combatant commands must protect oil assets and transportation routes – fighting tanker-hijacking pirates off the coast of Somalia or pipeline-attacking militants from Latin America to Central Asia. The US Army would love Mission Unnecessary in the Persian Gulf; the US Navy would no longer need to worry as much about conflicts from the Arctic to the South China Sea. Proliferators, meanwhile, could no longer hide their intent behind civilian nuclear power in a world that acknowledged its marketplace collapse and the superiority of nonnuclear competitors. Nor could they draw on civilian skills, materials, and equipment.

Phasing out fossil fuels would turbocharge global development, which is also in the United States' interest. Energy inefficiency is one of the biggest causes of persistent poverty. Oil purchases underlie much of the developing world's debt, and wasted energy diverts meagre national and household budgets. Developing countries are on average one-third as energy efficient as rich ones, and the poor often spend far more of their disposable income on energy than does the general population. Some 1.6 billion people live without electricity, leaving many basic needs unmet, hobbling health and development, and trapping women and girls in uneducated penury. Investments in new electricity devour one-fourth of the world's development capital. There is no stronger nor more neglected lever for global development than investing instead in making devices that save electricity. This would require about one-thousandth the capital and return it 10 times as fast, freeing up vast sums for other development needs. If the United States, Europe, China, and India merely adopted highly efficient lights, air conditioners, refrigerators, and TVs, they could save USD 1 trillion and 300 coal plants. That is the goal of the Super-efficient Equipment and Appliance Deployment Initiative, an effort announced in 2009 and supported by 23 major countries.

Developing countries, with their rural villages, burgeoning cities and slums, and dilapidated infrastructures, especially need renewable electricity, and they now buy the majority of the world's new renewable capacity. Some remote villages are not waiting for the wires but leapfrogging the grid: more Kenyans are getting electricity first from solar-power entrepreneurs than from traditional utilities. Such efforts as the US Department of Energy's Lumina Project have helped bring efficient and affordable solar-powered LED lights to millions across Africa. These projects improve education; free up kerosene budgets for mosquito nets, clean water, and other necessities; and could eventually prevent 1.5 million deaths from lung disease annually. Just by switching from kerosene lamps to fluorescent ones, one Indian village got 19 times as much light with one-ninth the energy and half the cost.

Getting unstuck
The United States cannot afford to keep waiting for a grid-locked Congress to act while the global clean-energy revolution passes it by. While US fossil-fuel industries guard their parochial interests, Denmark is planning to get entirely off fossil fuels by 2050; Sweden has even aimed for 2020. Germany's campaign for renewables and energy efficiency helped push unemployment in the country to its lowest rate in a decade. German Chancellor Angela Merkel is winning her bet that the Russian company Gazprom is a less worthy recipient of German energy expenditures than German engineers, manufacturers, and installers. Brazil, Japan, and South Korea, meanwhile, are catching up in renewables. India has passed Japan and the United Kingdom in renewables investments and aims to rival China's global leadership in the sector.

As Washington's clean-energy research-and-development budget has shrunk, Beijing's has soared. In 2005, China's 11th five-year plan made lower energy intensity the top strategic priority for national development. In 2010, the 12th five-year plan launched a USD 0.8 trillion decarbonisation effort, created the world's largest carbon-trading zone, and effectively capped China's carbon emissions. The country's net additions of coal plants fell by half between 2006 and 2010, and the overall efficiency of its coal plants pulled ahead of that of the United States'. No treaty compelled Beijing's leadership – just enlightened self-interest.

The United States' half-heartedness raises a conundrum: if the vision of an efficient clean-energy economy is so compelling, what keeps all US citizens, firms, and institutions from embracing it as vigorously as a few states have? The answer is that markets outpace understanding, disinformation and parochial politics abound, and the road remains strewn with barriers, myths, and pervasive favouritism for incumbents. But must Thucydides' lament become Americans' fate – that each politician pursues self-advantage while "the common cause imperceptibly decays"? The chief obstacle is not technology or economics but slow adoption. Helping innovations catch on will take education, leadership, and rapid learning. But it does not require reaching a consensus on motives. If Americans agree what should be done, then they need not agree why. Whether one cares most about national security, health, the environment, or simply making money, saving and supplanting fossil fuels makes sense.

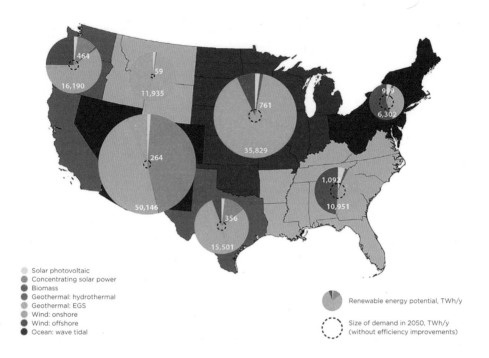

- Solar photovoltaic
- Concentrating solar power
- Biomass
- Geothermal: hydrothermal
- Geothermal: EGS
- Wind: onshore
- Wind: offshore
- Ocean: wave tidal

Renewable energy potential, TWh/y

Size of demand in 2050, TWh/y
(without efficiency improvements)

Figure 4 **Map showing US renewable energy potential**
Rocky Mountain Institute.

The potential capacity of renewable energy that can be harnessed by commercially available technologies is enormous. Even without widespread adoption of energy efficiency, the projected 2050 US electricity demand can be met many times over by renewables. Actual demand could be 10–45% lower after efficiency improvements. Additionally, each US region has the resource potential to meet well over 100% of its demand from renewable energy, thereby significantly reducing risks and costs associated with transmission development. As an example, the High Plains is one of the most wind-rich areas of the United States. But adding in the costs of losses of new lines hauling their power to distant regions would make them less competitive, perhaps uncompetitive, with resources nearby. Rather than building enormous long-distance transmission infrastructure to connect wind farms in this region to load centres spread around the country, local loads can be met by local resources in the Great Lakes, the Appalachians, and offshore on both coasts.

Rocky Mountain Institute © 2011. For more information see www.RMI.org/ReinventingFire.

Wise energy policy can grow from impeccably conservative roots – allowing and requiring all ways to save or produce energy to compete fairly at honest prices, regardless of their type, technology, size, location, or ownership. Who would oppose that? And what if the United States reversed the runaway energy-subsidy arms race, heading toward zero? Let those energy producers that insist they get no taxpayer largess explain why they are so loath to give it up.

Moving the United States off oil and coal will require Americans to trust in their own resourcefulness, ingenuity, and courage. These durable virtues can give the country fuel without fear; help set the world on a path beyond war, want, or waste; and turn energy from worrisome to worry-free, from risk to reward, from cost to profit.

CRADLE TO CRADLE®
FROM RECYCLING BUILDING COMPONENTS TO UP-CYCLING BUILDINGS. ADAPTING TO ACCELERATED BUILDING CYCLES

6

Douglas Mulhall and Michael Braungart

New technologies are allowing buildings to perform new services. This improves quality because it improves our lives and adds value for stakeholders. As part of improving the quality of buildings to make them healthier it makes sense to improve the quality of materials used in and recycled from buildings. However, oddly the materials used in buildings are often not designed for human contact. This negatively affects the quality of air and water and the total quality of buildings. Minimising those negative impacts is a start but the more practical approach is to maximise the beneficial footprint of a building. Buildings have a big footprint so the challenge is to make it beneficial. The Cradle to Cradle® Design paradigm provides a roadmap for achieving this quality. There is no Cradle to Cradle® building in the marketplace today but there are examples of Cradle to Cradle® Elements as first steps. This chapter examines the core principles and application tools associated with those examples.

Professor Dr Michael Braungart is co-founder of the award-winning Cradle to Cradle Design Protocol® and holds the Cradle to Cradle Chair at Erasmus University as well as a Chair at Twente University, and a visiting professorship at TU Delft, each in The Netherlands. He is founder and owner of EPEA Umweltforschung GmbH, based in Hamburg since 1987 and co-founder of McDonough Braungart Design Chemistry in Charlottesville, Virginia. He is a recipient of the USEPA Presidential Green Chemistry Challenge Award.

Douglas Mulhall developed residential housing in Canada, water recycling systems in China, and co-founded the Environmental Insitute in Brazil. He develops Cradle to Cradle® projects with EPEA Umweltforschung GmbH and is a researcher with Cradle to Cradle® institutes at Rotterdam School of Management, Technische Universität München and Delft University of Technology. He has co-authored various publications, including *Cradle to Cradle® Criteria for the Built Environment* and *The Guide to Cradle to Cradle in Buildings*.

epea@epea.com

Introduction

Buildings are gold mines of materials just waiting to be harvested, and if designed correctly they can be materials repleters instead of depleters. However, if you look at how most buildings are demolished you can quickly see that they are not designed for disassembly or materials recovery. If they were, it would be more economic to take them apart like a Lego set instead of smashing them to pieces then treating the remainder as waste.

Moreover, when buildings are renovated the resulting 'waste' is often classified as toxic, requiring special disposal methods and resulting in loss of valuable materials to the supply chain. The same applies to products and materials that are removed from buildings during their operations, including everything from heating ventilation and air conditioning (HVAC) components to the garbage that goes out the back door every day.

Businesses throw away hundreds of billions worth of valuable materials because they are not designed for recovery. What is gained on the front end through convenient bonding is lost on the back end through destructive mixing of materials that degrades their quality.

This has nothing to do with sustainability. It's just bad business and bad quality. Likewise, the solution has less to do with sustainability and more to do with quality assurance.

To try and solve something that is essentially a quality question, our 'sustainable' regulatory and ranking systems have focused on getting the wrong thing perfectly right.

The conventional approach of governments and industry has been to minimise the environmental impacts of their activities by being 'less bad' as products go from 'cradle to grave'.

This approach has allowed us to quantify the problem, but the resulting solutions have not been effective for many reasons. Foremost among those is the perception of cost. Sustainability is still often seen as involving extra costs for stakeholders without many benefits. Leaders talk about the importance of being sustainable, but in the background they regard it as an irritating cost, which in many cases it actually is. As a result, 'sustainability' has often prevented the use of quality assurance methods that are commonplace in most industries.

To solve this, the Cradle to Cradle Design Protocol® has taken a fundamentally different approach that generates benefits for stakeholders by going beyond the 'grave' and beyond conventional interpretations of 'environment' to promote quality assurance.

Cradle to Cradle® brief outline

Cradle to Cradle (C2C)[1] is a paradigm-changing innovation platform developed in the 1990s by Michael Braungart, William McDonough et al, based on research at the Environmental Protection Encouragement Agency in Hamburg, Germany, for designing beneficial economic, social and environmental features into products, processes and systems.

Cradle to Cradle® is primarily an entrepreneurial and innovation concept that starts by determining the intended benefits of a product or service instead of focusing on minimising negative environmental impacts.

To enhance quality and add value for stakeholders, C2C promotes innovation partnerships along the entire chain of a product, including manufacturing, distribution, use, disassembly, recovery and reuse.

By characterising hundreds of products and thousands of materials for their human and environmental health attributes, as well as defining systems to safely and fully cycle materials into new products, C2C has already provided a practical yet inspirational scientific and business model for improving quality.

This innovation and value model makes C2C potentially attractive to planners, builders and manufacturers for integration into products, processes, buildings, materials recovery systems, and purchasing.

Extensive books, cover stories and documentary films have been published and broadcasted about C2C since the 1990s. The book *Cradle to Cradle*[2] is well known and translated into at least a dozen languages.

However, many planners are not yet familiar with how to integrate into the built environment C2C features such as beneficial materials. There is a tendency when encountering well-known phrases such as 'safe materials' and 'species diversity', to respond with "yes, we do that already". But most buildings and area plans don't already do that. Methods are still not well established for designing sites so they contain defined materials, or are species-positive.

But this is changing. A rapid acceleration occurred from 2008 to 2013 in the numbers of planners, architects and engineers introducing C2C concepts into planning and construction. A priority expressed by government agencies is to translate C2C into renewal and new construction of buildings. Those requests resulted in our guidance booklet *Cradle to Cradle® Criteria for the Built Environment* (Mulhall & Braungart, 2010)[3].

It is not our purpose here to review those criteria, but instead to highlight preconditions that can be used by designers and builders in making buildings truly recyclable, and provide concrete examples of how Cradle to Cradle® elements are being included in buildings in practice.

Redefining recycling

If you want to get your materials back at the same level of quality, or sell them to other stakeholders at a profit, the first step is to redefine recycling, otherwise you end up selling contaminated waste instead of valuable materials.

The current definition of recycled content does not include defining that content, with the result that many materials cannot be recovered for use at the safe level of quality.

The definition of 'recycled content' could be improved by including these factors that describe the quality of a product and its component materials.

Content

What is in the recycled content? Are all contents known, especially additives that give materials such as paper, plastic, and metals added functional qualities?

• The material contains 'recycled' as distinguished from 'recyclable' content.

• In the case of recyclable content, the material has infrastructures in place for recovering that content.

• If the material contains 'biobased' content, this is distinguished clearly from 'biodegradable' content. Those terms are commonly confused. Biobased content does not mean a material is biodegradable, and biodegradable does not mean it is biobased. This is important for determining how the product will be disposed of or reused.

• For biodegradable content, the material can decompose in available biodegradation facilities, e.g., many biodegradable materials do not decompose fast enough in industrial composting facilities and are incinerated. To solve this the material is defined for industrial composting.

Intended Use and Defined Use

The Intended Use of a product defines what the product is intended to do for the customer. By defining functionality it is possible to consider innovations to improve Intended Use of a product. After Intended Use is defined and optimised, the Defined Use is determined. Defined use is the pathway the material follows through manufacturing, use, disposal and next use. By defining the use it is possible to design the materials for a biological pathway where they go directly into the environment as nutrients or go into a technical pathway where they are recovered at high quality for re-use. Cradle to Cradle technological and biological cycles are cited in many publications as being foundations for materials flows in the circular economy.

An example of Intended Use is a material intended to be used indoors as a floor covering. In this use the material might also perform an actively beneficial function, such as cleaning the air or generating renewable energy. An example is a floor covering that actively cleans the air. The product is on the market today.

An example of Defined Use is: in a technical cycle a material can contain toxic materials to perform a function. For example, many electronics products only function by using materials that are toxic if ingested. In C2C the key criteria is that those materials are safely locked into the material without being ingested through human contact or causing offgassing, and are recovered safely for reuse using available technologies.

Distinguishing between 'renewable' and 'recoverable'

Scaleability is an important criteria under Cradle to Cradle® when evaluating if a resource is renewable. For example, sometimes the recycling information on products includes a statement that the material comes from 'renewable' resources. However, it is just as important if and how the materials can be recovered and reused as nutrients.

For example some natural fibres start out as renewable but then become unsustainable when billions of people use them in their products. In Europe, wood was once renewable until governments subsidised burning it for energy, at which point it became rapidly unsustainable. By contrast, 'non-renewable' elements such as silver and gold can satisfy the requirements of billions of users if they are recovered and recycled effectively.

By paying attention to scaleability, the 'renewability' designation can be maintained when a product or process is rapidly scaled up, increasing demand versus supply for a given material.

Material integrity

• The material can be recycled at a similar level of quality, instead of being downcycled into lower quality products, e.g., from high quality engineering plastics into low quality park benches. In some cases the quality cannot be maintained, e.g., with paper, because fibres are destroyed during the recycling process. In those cases the question is, can the material be downcycled in a controlled 'cascade' so its uses are maximised? Separate publications are available describing the materials cascade. This is an important aspect because studies show that when biobased materials are used in cascades, the economic benefits far outweigh using them once then treating them as waste.

• The materials are assembled into the product in such a way that their integrity can be maintained when the product is disassembled.

• The material has a designated pathway for recycling at a similar level of quality.

With those important redefinitions in mind, here are examples of how Cradle to Cradle® elements are practically included in buildings.

Examples of Cradle to Cradle® elements in buildings

Designing for recycling biological nutrients

Designing buildings to be recyclable involves far more than just designing them to come apart. Many of the biobased products manufactured and used by our society pass through or are used in buildings, including paper, wood, food, textiles, and cleaners.

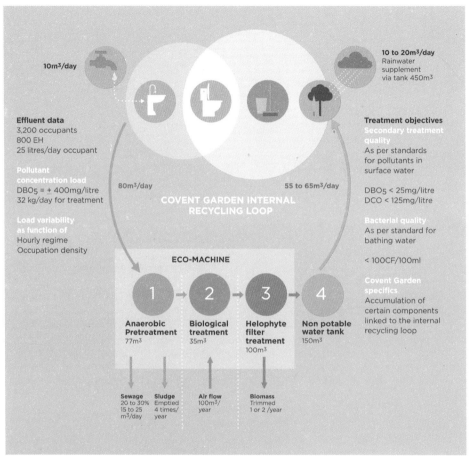

10 to 20m³/day
Rainwater
supplement
via tank 450m³

10m³/day

Effluent data
3,200 occupants
800 EH
25 litres/day occupant

**Pollutant
concentration load**
DBO5 = + 400mg/litre
32 kg/day for treatment

**Load variability
as function of**
Hourly regime
Occupation density

80m³/day

**COVENT GARDEN INTERNAL
RECYCLING LOOP**

55 to 65m³/day

Treatment objectives
**Secondary treatment
quality**
As per standards
for pollutants in
surface water

DBO5 < 25mg/litre
DCO < 125mg/litre

Bacterial quality
As per standard for
bathing water

< 100CF/100ml

**Covent Garden
specifics**
Accumulation of
certain components
linked to the internal
recycling loop

ECO-MACHINE

1 → 2 → 3 → 4

**Anaerobic
Pretreatment**
77m³

**Biological
treatment**
35m³

**Helophyte
filter
treatment**
100m³

**Non potable
water tank**
150m³

Sewage
20 to 30%
15 to 25
m³/day

Sludge
Emptied
4 times/
year

Air flow
100m³/
year

Biomass
Trimmed
1 or 2 /year

Figure 1 **Covent Garden internal recycling loop**

Figure 2 **Covent Garden and
Eco-Machine Brussels**
(Art & Build Architects/
Steven Beckers and Montois
Partners Architects.
Photographer:Serge Brison)

Yet most buildings are not designed to reuse those nutrients, and so they pass out the back end as waste.

However, buildings like Covent Garden in Brussels have been designed to reprocess their own biological nutrients from water effluent.

The 75,000m sq office building is designed to be nearly autonomous in water by combination of biological water treatment (800 equivalent inhabitant) and use of rainwater. Treated water is used to flush toilets and for cleaning and irrigation. Resulting sludge and phosphate are used as fertilizer. The system is integrated under the atrium, with simple anaerobic treatment receiving all grey and black waters followed by membrane filtering. Polishing of the water happens through successive passage into the roots of atrium plantings before being stored for use alongside rainwater storage. Resulting water is of 'bathing quality' and necessitates no chemicals. The approach is being optimised during operations.

Integrating design for disassembly with multiple beneficial functions
Architects are proving it is possible to go beyond just design for disassembly by integrating multiple beneficial C2C elements into buildings.

This is elegantly illustrated in the William McDonough + Partners Architects design for the Visitor Center, Bernheim Arboretum and Research Forest, Clermont, Kentucky, which uses recycled wood, geothermal heating and cooling, and a system in which roofwater is reused for toilets. The building, which is situated in a forest, is designed to come apart: It employs simple connectors, the wood can be reused or returned to the soil, and the steel is also easily removable and reusable. This design for disassembly strategy is important because it enables the reuse of things to the greatest extent possible (no lost areas damages during de-installation), and because it reduces waste stream (no joints sent to landfill). It also makes sure things can be recycled. For example, with a wood joist floor, you can unscrew and recycle/upcycle/compost/reuse.

Figure 3 **Visitor Center, Bernheim Arboretum and Research Forest, Clermont, Kentucky** (William McDonough + Partners)

In the NASA Sustainability Base project, the selection of steel over concrete structure and the componentising of the exterior wall lend themselves to disassembly detailing. The exoskeleton approach offers increased structural performance during seismic events, provides an armature for daylighting and shading strategies, and creates a column-free interior that facilitates workplace flexibility. It also becomes the icon for the building, recalling lunar modules and satellites. Other project innovations range from aggressive daylighting and natural ventilation design to in-depth materials screening. The resulting building will be a flexible workplace filled with glare-free daylight, fresh air and abundant connections to the outdoors, serviced by systems that, in time, will use only renewable energy and will maintain water in closed loops.

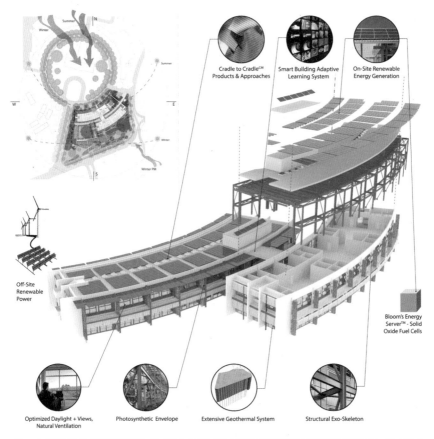

Figure 4 **NASA Sustainability Base Ames Research Center California** (William McDonough + Partners)

At the Berlaymont, European Commmission Headquarters in Brussels, a disassemblable glass facade performs multiple functions; Designed to protect the existing steel suspended structure from overheating, plus protection from weather and cold nights, the automated louvered glass facade provides 300% additional natural light for only 13% energy transfer. Natural light is diffused by the louvers through the clear glass curtain wall without chromatic transformation thanks to the use of screen printed polyethylene terephthalate (known as PET) film inserted in the laminated glass. One-way vision is ensured by white dots printed on black dots allowing vision from inside and reflection.

Figure 5 **European Commmission Headquarters, Brussels**
(Architects: Steven Beckers and Pierre Lallemand, Berlaymont 2000 sa. Detrois)

Figure 6 **Venlo City Hall, The Netherlands** (Kraaijvanger Urbis)

Venlo City Hall takes the facade approach one step further by including vegetation that performs multiple functions such as particulate metabolisation, temperature moderation, and water capture. Instead of purifying air from the outside coming in, the design is to clean air from the inside coming out. Facades are easily maintained and removable features that can integrate multiple functions. Furthermore, planners meet monthly with suppliers to discuss how C2C features can most effectively be included in the building. This is a novel approach to marketplace inspiration by governments.

Designing material partnerships
Imagine if you were able to design buildings where manufacturers have a mechanism to own and maintain the materials so there is an incentive to design their products to be profitably recovered. Imagine the capital cost savings to building owners. Imagine the advantages to manufacturers if they could get scarce resources back without relying on raw materials providers in volatile commodities markets.

That 'imagine' is being practiced right now in Amsterdam by Rau Architects. The architectural firm is 'walking the walk' at its own offices through product leasing arrangements with suppliers.

• Lighting is leased from Philips. Instead of selling lights, the company started to lease lighting on the request of Rau, based on an approach pioneered by EPEA Internationale Umweltforschung.

Figure 7 **RAU office, Netherlands**

• C2C certified® furniture (tables, chairs) by Steelcase.

• C2C certified® Floor tiles by Desso, a company that also offers microfibres that actively clean the air.

• C2C certified® ceramic tiles by Mosa in the restrooms.

• As well, Rau has service contracts with companies such as Van Houtum for C2C certified® sanitary paper, and Van Ganssewinkel and Oce for C2C certified® printer paper. Those biological nutrients are designed for the biological cycle.

"I don't want to own products, all I'm interested in is the performance a product offers," says architect Thomas Rau. His Rau office has been completely redesigned with products that not only remain the property of the producer, but will also be taken back at the end of the contract for reuse in a new generation of products. "This performance-based service does not only relieve me of the responsibility to dispose of products at the end of their life span, it stimulates reuse of raw materials and drives innovation."

The concept of 'performance-based consumption' is a promising application of the Cradle to Cradle® paradigm, simply maintaining raw materials in a technical nutrient cycle.

Acknowledgements

Appreciation to Kira Gould, William McDonough + Partners, Steven Beckers and Art & Build Architects, Kaan Ozdurak, Thomas Rau Architects for providing images and captions.

Notes

1 *Various iterations of 'Cradle to Cradle' and 'C2C' are registered marks of McDonough Braungart Design Chemistry*

2 *Cradle to Cradle. Remaking the Way We Make Things. William McDonough & Michael Braungart, North Point Press NY, 2002*

3 *Cradle to Cradle® Criteria for the Built Environment, Douglas Mulhall & Michael Braungart, CEO media, The Netherlands, 2010. http://www.duurzaamgebouwd.nl/20101007-cradle-to-cradle-criteria-for-the-built-environment*

BUSINESS OPPORTUNITIES THROUGH POSITIVE DEVELOPMENT

7

Janis Birkeland

The built environment mirrors the linear economy and concretises the ecological and ethical deficits caused by the dominant industrial paradigm of development. An alternative paradigm, called Positive Development (PD) reverses the dominant paradigm (DP) on all levels. It replaces DP's binary decision systems, linear and reductionist analyses, zero sum decision frameworks and negative thinking with a positive and open systems design framework. There are limits of industrial growth, but there are no limits to positive forms of economic, social and environmental growth. Here we focus on 'positive retrofitting' – a business gold mine. This chapter explains: why sustainability is a design problem; why 'green buildings' are not yet sustainable; what constitutes a sustainable built environment; how cities can drive PD through eco-positive retrofitting; and how to start by mapping ethical business opportunities.

Janis Birkeland (retired) was most recently Professor of Sustainable Design at the School of Architecture and Planning, University of Auckland. She is Adjunct Professor at Queensland University of Technology (QUT). Janis is author of Positive Development - from vicious circles to virtuous cycles through built environment design.

janis.lynn.Birkeland@gmail.com

Introduction

A circular economy will require a fundamental change in not only manufacturing but in the planning and design of cities. Modern cities and buildings have been designed on the model of 20th-century factories, sucking living and mineral resources from their regions in a one-directional and terminal process. Construction systems are segregated, linear processes that convert resources into wastes. In fact, virtually all environmental health and sustainability issues can be linked to the design of the 'built environment' (infrastructure, buildings, landscapes, products, etc.). Globally, for example, buildings alone are responsible for about 40% of energy consumption and over 30% of carbon emissions, while cities as a whole are accountable for 75% of carbon emissions (Un-Habitat, 2011). Further, the design of cities and built environments drive the demand upon primary industries for manufactured goods, and these invariably produce far fewer resources than are used to produce them. Even 'zero waste' to landfill has addressed a tiny fraction of the waste downstream or upstream of manufacturing (Hawken, 1993).

Sustainability was originally about life quality: making everyone in the present and future better off (IUCN/UNEP/WWF, 1980). As presently designed, the on-going negative impacts of even 'green' buildings are more than cancelling out their life quality and lifestyle benefits. They are not sustainable because, among other things, they are steadily destroying the life support system (nature), increasing the disparity of wealth, and limiting adaptability and future proofing (UNEP, 2012). Urban development and design does not yet even attempt to compensate for increases in global population, poverty and pollution, or for losses in biodiversity, productive land and water. Yet even if the human population crashes, we will need to address these ecological and ethical deficits and increase ecological carrying capacity – just to stand still. That is, development must be net positive before cities can become impact neutral.

Box 1 provides a sampling of 'environmental' problems that are caused or exacerbated by built environment planning and design. Fortunately, these can be reversed by Positive Development (PD). PD posits that existing cities can be retrofitted to remove their on-going negative impacts and also generate ecologically and socially net positive impacts (Birkeland, 2008). Net positive cities are possible due to the unique potential of design to create multifunctional structures and spaces that support both nature and society. PD would decouple economic growth from environmental impacts, but this requires a paradigm shift well beyond that envisaged by the literature of 'sustainable development'. Leading-edge design still only aims to regenerate damaged ecosystems, not to increase ecosystems and ecological carrying capacity in absolute terms (Box 3). A net PD would go further than zero impact or regenerative design by increasing both:

• The 'ecological base' – a term encompassing ecosystem goods and services, natural capital, biodiversity habitats, ecological health and resilience, bio-security, etc. (or the intrinsic and instrumental values of nature).

• The 'public estate', as substantive democracy ultimately depends on equitable access to, and the expansion of, the means of survival, and especially in crises.

Efforts to quantify the net positive ecological impacts of buildings have begun (Renger, Birkeland & Midmore, 2013). However, achieving net positive life cycle impacts is easier in the case of retrofitting. Here we examine why 'Eco-positive retrofitting' is an ethical business opportunity that can make everyone better off. To that end, this chapter explains: (a) why sustainability is a design problem; (b) why green buildings and eco-cities are not yet sustainable; (c) what would constitute a sustainable urban built environment; (d) how urban planning and design can become net positive; (e) why Eco-positive retrofitting is a business gold mine; and (f) how to start.

Box 1 Some urban problems caused by design

There are several things to note about the urban design problems listed below: (a) they are all caused by development and not by nature; (b) they could all be prevented or mitigated by built environment design; (c) being a by-product of design, they are under human control, and thus a collective social responsibility; and (d) fixing these systemic design issues would help the economy as well as the society and environment.

• Built environment design aggravates risks to human safety from weather, floods, mould, radon and so on. For example, the urban heat island effect can contribute to cyclones, floods, lightening, and fires. Planning and design can mitigate, neutralise or even utilise most natural forces (except for meteorites).

• The design of centralised and linear systems of industrial infrastructure (power, electricity, transport, sewerage, water, etc.) can cause blackouts, gridlock, soil contamination from leaky water and sewerage pipes, storm water run-off, and toxic dust from fossil fuels and mining.

• Current urban density and design reduces survival options and escape routes, especially in crises like earthquakes, fuel shortages or warfare. In many cities around the world today, impoverished urban civilians live as if locked in medieval fortresses under siege.

• In disadvantaged regions, people that move to cities to seek work often remain homeless and in poverty. The increasing urban population will need more food, water, air, mobility, etc. just to maintain current negative levels of social and ecological problems.

• In over-developed countries, urban design is complicit in the spread of disease, obesity and a growing lack of motor coordination in children. Many people feel safer in cars designed like weapons which may protect the occupants, but not the millions of people that cars have killed.

• Millions born in disadvantaged nations or regions die prematurely every year from poor sanitation, water and air, even though low-cost eco-technologies already exist for treating, reusing and distributing these essential services (Living Machines, Solar Cones or water-filtering bicycles and wheelbarrows, etc.).

• Whether compact or dispersed in form, cities deplete their bioregions of materials, energy, fertile land and essential ecosystems. The on-going impact of past construction and renovation due to the design of buildings and cities take from nature without giving anything back.

• Total waste is increasing per capita as the population grows geometrically. Even if the population crashes, reliance of fossil fuels could mean escalating geopolitical conflict, continuing bioaccumulation of toxins in the air, water and soil, and greater concentrations of wealth and power.

• While central business districts are exciting and even glamorous, cities are also a hotbed of social, political and economic strife and disparities, and much of their peripheries are depressingly grey, dirty and monotonous. The opportunity costs of poor urban design are incalculable.

Background

There are many systemic reasons for the failure of cities in terms of sustainability. One of these is the disconnect between business, industry and built environment design, although integration is progressing. Over recent decades, there has been a shift in thinking from terminal to circular patterns of production that recycle waste into resources. These have been theorised as urban and industrial metabolism (Boyden et al., 1981; Wolman, 1965; Ayres & Simonis, 1994; Tibbs, 2002) and have materialised into closed-loop manufacturing systems (Stahel, 2013; McDonough & Braungart, 2002) and even cross-sectoral loops, such as urban organic waste to farms (Gillespie, 2008) or farm waste to factories using 'Living Machines' (Todd & Todd, 1994). Today, architects and engineers can specify more sustainable building products and materials to replace harmful ones and reduce natural resources per unit of production. Specification tools are now available which rank building products and materials according to their life cycle impacts (e.g. www.ecospecifier.com.au). These can give a well-deserved advantage to green/good businesses. However, there is still a long way to go. If a product or structure designed to be like an ecosystem is redundant, lacks a good public purpose, or contributes to increased consumption overall, it can still do more harm than good (Harrison et al., 2002; Hill, 2002).

Moreover, a zero-waste, closed-loop system seldom produces natural resources or 'eco-services'. Eco-services are the myriad ecosystem goods, services and values that natural systems provide virtually for free (Beattie & Ehrlich, 2004). Eco-services are crucial to life itself, so they are the life blood of sustainability. Because built environment decision systems are dominated by numerical formulas and cost benefit frameworks, design, ecology and ethics – which go to the heart of sustainability – have largely been excluded. For example, sustainable development frameworks and tools have only measured negative (or less negative) impacts. Therefore, developers and designers have had little information or incentives for generating net positive environmental and social outcomes. PD is based on the recognition that society, nature and cities are complex systems requiring not only closed-loop engineering and manufacturing, but open systems design that generates virtuous cycles throughout society.

Since eco-positive design is not yet on the radar, one might ask: "how is it possible for development to generate net positive ecological outcomes, instead of just reducing negative impacts?" One of the things that differentiates manufacturing from built environment design is space. Space is central in the training of architects and planners, but often forgotten in practice. It does not in itself consume energy or cost money, and it can be framed and weatherproofed with low-impact structures and materials. Design, using space, can create an experiential 'wow factor'. At the same time, public space can lessen the impacts of disparities of wealth, health and environmental amenity, and replace the need for 'defensive' expenditures on security, privacy, and various material substitutes for psychological well-being. Existing urban areas offer the vertical space and infrastructure for growing surplus ecological carrying capacity, ecosystems and eco-services in multi-functional 'gardens for living' that support nature and people synergistically, called 'Ecological Space'.

There are of course systemic barriers to an eco-positive paradigm and practice, but these should not be difficult to overcome. The misconception still exists that green design costs more, and design is still often seen as decoration, or even an extravagance (Box 2). But many studies have refuted this view (Kats, 2005; GBCA, 2006 ; Esty & Wilston, 2006). The fact is, assuming good design, the more sustainable a building is, the less it costs society and owners (Weizsacker, Lovins & Lovins, 1997; Wann, 1996). Conventional buildings are actually more costly in full-cost-pricing terms, as they have irreversible impacts over their life cycle in all dimensions of sustainability: economic, environmental, ecological and ethical. Sometimes green buildings have 'extra' R&D costs, but these can be recouped through resource savings in a few years (Edwards, 1998).

Box 2 **Biases against design**

There are many reasons, other than the misconceptions about costs, that people still under-value built environment design as a means to sustainability. Some of these are as follows:

• The dominant industrial paradigm and linear economy have been projected onto and concretised by modern cities. This makes cities seem normal. The wealthy seldom 'see' the ugly parts of cities, as these do not affect their life quality. Those eking out a living in impoverished and high crime areas cannot be expected to associate built environment design with health, safety and security.

• There are few if any eco-positive built environments to experience. People cannot be expected to imagine good design in the vast array of our noisy, polluted and over-crowded urban environments. Even green renditions of buildings are often sterile, single-function urban cages that create 'dead' left-over spaces.

• In the context of a linear economy, all construction uses resources, so it is easy to forget that building-integrated eco-services can potentially produce natural capital (aquaponics, vertical wetlands, algaetecture, permaculture, etc.). Our society still sees design as something to be applied at the end of the line to decorate industrial engineering, not something that can expand future options by increasing the life support system.

• Buildings are largely composed of manufactured products. In most manufacturing systems, one cannot do better than 'closing resource loops' or recycling throughout each stage of the production process. Industrial fabrication always entails some energy and waste, even in recycling processes and, therefore, has negative ecological impacts. In fact, 'up-cycling' waste from one process or product into higher uses usually refers only to economic values, not ecological value.

• The built environment and design have been marginalised by the dominant paradigm that assumes nature and development are zero-sum or can be 'balanced', rather than be symbiotic and synergistic. Development controls, in effect, balance off the immediate environmental damage of each development within limited systems boundaries against its economic benefits.

• Economic and social benefits for humans from design, such as thermal comfort, free energy, clean air, worker productivity, are often counted as ecological 'gains', and yet are used, in effect, to offset negative impacts on the ecological base.

• We choose not to measure the positive impacts of design, which devalues the benefits of design. Also our assessment tools exclude many negative impacts (identified by SMARTmode), so we do not appreciate that sustainable development assessments address only a fraction of environmental problems.

Errors in green design can of course create extra costs, such as tacking green equipment onto the conventional building prototype, or underutilising passive solar design principles. But it should be remembered that green buildings did not get the hundred years of subsidies that conventional 'fossil fuelled' buildings enjoyed during their evolution. Annual subsidies to renewables reportedly only exceeded that given to fossil fuels in 2010. "Over the full lifetime of subsidies, the oil and gas industry has benefitted from tax expenditures of, on average, USD 4.86 billion per year between 1918 and 2009. The renewables industry has received an average of only USD 0.37 billion per year between 1994 and 2009." (Yale Center for Business and Environment, 2012). The confusion about costs is because industrial and sustainable buildings are not yet compared on a level playing field. For example, green design and technologies must pay for themselves, while fossil fuels never pay back their costs, let alone their environmental and health externalities. Likewise, the maintenance costs of passive or natural systems like living walls or roofs are seen as a maintenance problem, yet the maintenance costs of fossil-fuel-based building (e.g. cleaning curtain glass walls) are ignored or treated as a neutral baseline.

Why sustainability depends on systems design

In this section, we look at how economic, social and ecological sustainability are ultimately dependent on the ecological base and how, in each case, the ecological base depends on systems design. Hence, sustainability depends on design (Figure 1). The point is that since poor design has caused such problems, and design is a unique human capability and responsibility, humans must correct their past design errors.

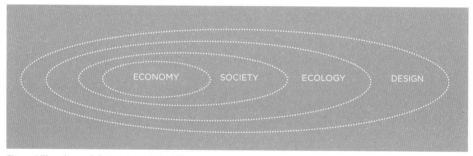

Figure 1 **The place of design in sustainability**

Economic dependence on the ecological base and design

Most economists recognise that the economy, let alone humans, would not exist without the ecological base. Few, however, appear to be aware of the impacts of ecological losses upon the economy itself. The costs to the economy of poor systems design, manifested in climate change, pollution, waste, resource depletion, urban heat island effect and so on, generally exceed the financial gains to developers (Hamilton, 1994; HM Treasury, 2006). These design inefficiencies and ethical deficiencies accumulate costs that eventually rebound on all business and industry. These costs are designed in by economic constructs, so they are not really 'external' to the economy at all. However, the accountancy frameworks used in business, economics and even environmental management, have concealed these costs to the economy by isolating them in reductionist and often myopic tools.

Paradoxically, the solution to every 'economic' problem is assumed to be stimulating business and industry by moving money around. However, we have long known that public expenditures to stimulate business have often created perverse subsidies that destroy the things in life that were meant to be free (Repetto & Gillis, 1988; Myers & Kent, 2001). It is financial systems that impede positive change, rather than a lack of money. There is plenty of money to correct world problems if diverted from military spending. Many studies over the decades have shown that protecting existing natural functions and eco-services costs less than trying to replace them with industrial or mechanical substitutes (Heal, 2000). Melbourne and New York, for example, preserved lands in their catchment areas to treat water for millions of dollars less per year than an industrial water treatment plant would have cost, even counting the profits of selling off the timber (Daily & Ellison, 2002).

Economic growth is closely tied to the construction industry. If one excludes arms dealing, the oil industry and various highly profitable illegal activities, the construction industry ranks near the top of economic drivers. Of these, the built environment may be a better investment, as it is usually legal and profitable, and buildings do not skip the country. It has been shown that design can be the biggest factor in the profit margins of stakeholders, both through resource savings and value adding. After all, design represents only about 1% of the life cycle cost of a building, yet an investment in design upfront could save 90% energy over the life cycle (Hawken, Lovins & Lovins, 1999). Furthermore, it has long been known that healthy work environments are cheaper than the costs of shortened work life spans, medical treatment, loss of productivity, absenteeism and worker compensation (Romm, 1999).

The national benefits of good built environment design would be huge. A 10% savings in construction costs would have significant positive impacts on the economy and increase gross domestic product (GDP) by 3% (CSIRO, 1989). Remarkably, GDP is still the official indicator of economic growth, despite its flaws being explained in a speech by US Senator Robert F Kennedy in 1968 (see also Waring, 1998). In the context of GDP, which only counts financial transactions, 'efficiency' has meant downsizing the costs of production, like reducing employment, to produce more consumer goods and services. It is also well known that the assessment of the positive potential of design to economic wellbeing is skewed by the under-pricing of natural resources. However, in the current price-based and supply-driven economy, there is little chance of GDP being replaced by genuine progress indicators or full-cost pricing. Even these largely ignore the ecology, or treat units of money, carbon or energy as a surrogate for living ecosystems. Therefore, true economic performance in a whole system context will depend more on design than market signals or price-based indicators.

Social dependence on the ecological base and design
It is now widely understood, and reinforced by complexity and quantum theories, that everything is interconnected. We are all affected by the built environment, as nature, nurture, and environment cannot really be separated. Some urban residents may have become desensitised, but environmental or sensory deprivation can cause them mental and emotional disorders ('the gilded cage syndrome'). Therefore, psychological and social well-being, such as community belonging and sense of place, are inextricably linked to the design of the physical and natural environment (Wilson,

1993). In fact, most urban health problems can be linked to 'design for industrialism'. The sick building syndrome (well known by the 1990s), and the heat island effect (known by 1818), can be traced to industrial building systems.

Until recently, the reductionist sciences were unable or unwilling to measure the social impacts of design, such as the health benefits of greenery and natural daylight, as people did not fit into petri dishes. Increasingly, however, the ability to compare stress levels in people experiencing natural and urban environments has shown the importance of nature and its amenities to health (Schmidt, 2010). At a more fundamental level, the baseline of social sustainability is survival, security and health, and these require a reasonable degree of health and social equity (Marmot, 2004). Democracy is never guaranteed when there are disparities of benefits and burdens, or inequities in access to the means of health and survival. Injustice eventually leads to destructive forms of conflict, which are incompatible with social, ethical, economic or environmental sustainability.

Many urban planning and architecture courses and texts have stressed the social and psychological dimensions of design in making building users better off. Social goals seldom materialise in the final construction, however, since practice is largely driven by competition, market prices and stakeholder value. The outcomes of harsh economic and built environments are seen as social problems instead of the impacts of poor systems design. Similarly, building science methods have tended to side-line social, ecological and design elements and to target problems that can be expressed as inputs and outputs across a building envelope. Due to the dominance of 'decision making' (comparing and choosing among options using cost-benefit thinking), we do the cheapest thing that appears to outweigh the costs, rather than multiplying benefits by design.

Recently, given vast social and economic impacts of increasing 'natural' disasters, there has been an emphasis in planning and design for 'future proofing'. Yet little attention is paid to addressing the causes of these disasters in previous urban planning and design. Less is done to create positive synergies between buildings and the natural environment. For example, 'risk-benefit analyses' tend to locate a spot on the spectrum between risks and benefits which, in the real world, translates into 'balancing' money and risks. This is gambling, rather than pro-actively designing out risks. After all, a hundred year flood can occur twice in the first year. Built environment planning, design and retrofitting could prevent such risks from disasters in ways that also create ethical businesses and increase universal life quality. However, design is not well understood by those looking at balance sheets. Eco-positive design would have surplus benefits as well as resource savings, which would change the scales and equilibrium point of assessment entirely.

Ecological dependence on design
It takes about 1,000 sq km of varied ecosystems to support 1 sq km of a modern city (Wackernagel and Rees, 1996; Folke et al., 1997). That is, the ecological footprint (EF), the equivalent land and water consumed to support society, is about 1,000 to 1. In biodiversity offset systems, designed to compensate for 'approved' damage to the environment, the development footprint (i.e. ground coverage) is used instead

of the EF. That means, in a sense, offset schemes address 0.01% of the problem. When land is protected or restored, it is not an actual increase, as it already existed. Even when a smaller EF reduces some of the public costs externalised by development, such as embodied materials, waste and energy, this does not usually protect or increase ecological carrying capacity. EFs are averages which conceal their dependence on site-specific design. For instance, tall buildings with smaller spaces per person may take up less ground area than low-rise buildings, yet have a larger EF.

The EF depends on design and, without a new kind of design, neither low nor high density cities will protect or increase the life support system. Changing the paradigm and its systems will always involve upfront costs – even though a new green system will be more profitable. We count the 'sunk cost' or prior investment in negative systems when considering environmental protection, but not in 'rational' business decisions. Upfront costs of sustainable systems are easily addressed by financial mechanisms, as discussed in Box 5. Therefore, there is no point going through incremental changes or reinventing wheels. To move directly to net Positive Development, it is important to be clear about what is 'sustainable' and what is 'less un-sustainable'. To that end, we distinguish different levels of green buildings (Box 3).

What constitutes a 'sustainable' development
The key to understanding PD is the benchmark: pre-industrial ecology. The PD 'Sustainability Standard' is the required increase in the ecological base of the region and/or site (in relation to total floor area or the ecological footprint) as opposed to typical buildings. Ecological 'gains' cannot be relative to the current situation because, for example, de-contaminating a site or area with a development, however challenging, would only be remedial. 'Eco-positive' therefore means increases in ecological carrying capacity, eco-services, and other criteria relative to pre-industrial conditions over the life cycle. This does not mean a return to earlier conditions, of course, as the pre-industrial ecology could not support the current human population. The life support system must be increased to match increasing material flows.

Positive Development criteria
PD objectives follow logically from this standard to:
• reduce total resource flows over a building's life cycle;
• reverse the impacts of the growing disparity of wealth and life quality;
• increase ecological carrying capacity beyond pre-industrial conditions;
• generate surplus 'eco-services' in relation to floor area as well as ground area;
• produce net positive sustainability impacts beyond the given site or system borders;
• replace fossil-fuel-based mechanisms with passive and natural systems where possible;
• design reversible, adaptable, demountable and/or biodegradable systems;
• compensate for past design decisions and their environmental impacts;
• future proof the urban environment to reduce risks of flooding, earthquakes and so on;
• celebrate the intrinsic values of nature;
• create an urban gene bank for regenerating the bioregion.
(For PD design criteria, see Birkeland, 2008, p257-258)

Box 3 **Current architectural design models**

Note: These types of design overlap in time and are not chronological.

Green buildings: From the turn of this century, green design principles, most of which existed by the 1970s (Johnson, 1979; Papanek, 1971), have been adopted in formal design guidelines and rating tools. Today, 'green buildings' are those that rank on assessment tool score cards. Rating tools can increase the transaction costs of development, but still save money and reduce externalities that would otherwise be borne by the community. Green buildings are profitable (Kok, 2009), but do more harm than good to the ecology. In fact, some buildings with high ratings barely surpass minimum energy code requirements due to 'point scoring' (Safamanesh & Byrd, 2012). These tools were based on conventional (code compliant) buildings and reflect the legacy of the resource and capital intensive 'International Style', where universal design patterns replaced more climatically-sensitive designs. Such 'energy-efficient' building systems under-utilise passive systems design and will soon need to be retrofitted.

Passive solar: In many climates, the 'operating' energy required for heating, cooling and ventilating buildings (currently about 20% of total national energy usage) can be provided by passive solar design. Passive systems were popular in the 1960s and 1970s (AIA, 1976; Shurcliff, 1979). They use building form, local materials and natural forces (e.g., convection, conduction, evaporation and radiation) to capture, store and distribute the sun's 'free' energy. Given their use of organic materials, they are usually healthier, and easily modified. Being site specific, passive design can inspire interesting and diverse living environments (Corbett & Corbett, 1999). Passive design can conform to any style, but usually aims to look like a 'typical building'. Since passive solar design is usually applied in a tokenistic manner, it still requires back-up systems. Passive solar design does not yet aim to compensate for its impacts on the life support system.

Zero carbon/energy: Passive and resource autonomous buildings have been around for ages (Rudolfsky, 1967; Vale & Vale, 1975), and yet zero carbon or high-end green buildings are often presented as a new. Zero energy buildings have long been possible, apart from energy for computers and appliances for which solar cells can be used. However, zero carbon buildings usually just focus on operating energy, which is about half the energy used by buildings, or 20% of total national energy use (Crawford & Treloar, 2005). Embodied energy would be a much greater proportion of energy use if passive solar systems were maximised. Due to the 'International Style', many zero carbon buildings also tend to be minimalist, using single-function products, spaces and building forms which reduce their potential to regenerate the ecology, or protect critical ecosystems.

Regenerative design: Regenerative design aims to restore and sometimes increase the site's ecology, revitalise the community and, in theory, make urban areas more resilient (Lyle, 1994; McLennan, 2004). It is also beginning to integrate the ethical and ecological insights of other branches of sustainability (BRI, 2012; LBC, 2010). However, terms like 'resilience' or 'regeneration' are invariably used to mean design that leaves the community and environment 'better than it was' just before construction. This is not a solution to the accelerating resource and biodiversity losses that will eventually affect everyone. To be sustainable in the present planetary context, buildings will need to increase ecosystem carrying capacity to (over) compensate for the ecological footprint and various forms of embodied waste created in construction. This leads us to net Positive Development (PD).

Council House 2 in Melbourne, Australia, retrofitted an old building with numerous passive energy systems to save resources and energy while providing fresh air and environmental amenity. (Hugh Byrd)

Central Park Apartments in Sydney, Australia, now has the tallest vertical gardens. Green wall panels hold over 100,000 plants to provide inner city residents some contact with nature (Dominique Hes)

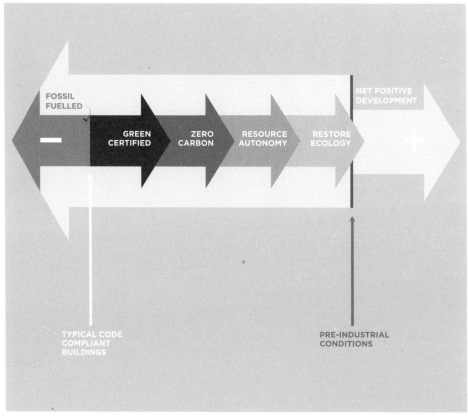

Figure 2 **Spectrum from typical to eco-positive design**

Design for Eco-services

'Design for Eco-services' is a key component of Positive Development (Birkeland, 2002). It means designing for nature as well as people, by enlisting biological systems and natural forces to create synergies through multi-functional, multi-sectoral and multi-scalar design – often in shared 'Ecological Space'. Building-integrated natural systems can mitigate the climate, sequester carbon, and provide dozens of eco-services, including clean energy, oxygen, food, water, materials and pollination (Box 4). The new reality is that we can no longer protect 'nature' in reserves outside of cities. Some reasons why environmental protection must happen in cities, as well as elsewhere, include the following:

• No land reserves or wilderness areas are actually 'protected'. As pressures build, protected land will eventually be re-allocated to development through the political/ market process.

• Nature preserves can no longer be protected from toxic dust, genetically-modified organisms, feral species and transnational corporations, as these know no boundaries.

• Even if we could isolate nature, we could not make relatively 'natural' areas more eco-productive, without destroying complex ecological systems that we do not understand.

• We pretend that we can neutralise ecological damage by long lasting buildings that amortise their energy usage but this, again, confuses ecology and energy.

One might argue that we could increase ecosystem services in rural areas, as degraded agricultural lands could become more productive and diverse. In some places, farms can now earn credits for restoring land to biodiversity preserves, and urban development can earn credits by protecting bits of land or restoring natural areas outside cities. However, rural regeneration is not likely to achieve a net increase in appropriate ecosystems or a net gain in land area for nature beyond pre-industrial conditions. Even assuming vast improvements in forestry, farming, fishing, factories and fuels, cities will still need to increase total ecological carrying capacity and eco-services to support the current urban human population sustainably. Eventually, rural areas may use vertical structures for some food products to take the pressure off native flora and fauna or even support them (e.g. create animal nesting places and food sources) – but this rural land would then be urban.

Box 4 **Examples of Design for Eco-services**

Many low-tech and natural systems can be integrated with urban structures and infrastructure to create eco-positive flows (see Birkeland, 2009 a & b). Passive solar systems, organic healthy materials and natural air and water filtration systems are inherently cheaper than their industrial counterparts. The following are random examples:

• 'Green scaffolding' is like a space frame that is multi-functional and multi-scalar, and can transform existing environments into net positive systems (Birkeland, 2008). It can support at least 35 eco-services and can be adapted to any situation or orientation (Birkeland 2013b)

• 'Algaetecture' uses transparent tubes arranged on a sun-lit structure that consume CO_2 while producing biomass and oxygen. It can produce biofuels and Omega 3 without competing with land for food. Such structures can be combined with wind or PV systems, building facades, biodiversity habitat, and so on (see www.algaeindustry.com or http://www.algaetecture.com/)

• 'Biotecture' uses microbes to perform functions like repairing and cleaning building facades or producing light and oxygen. In theory microbes could stop the spread of deserts by using bacteria to turn dunes into habitable sandstone structures (Larsson, 2008). The structure creates a cooler interior which can support dew harvesting, permaculture, living space and thermal comfort. http://www.treehugger.com/clean-technology/could-bacteria-filled-balloons-stop-the-spread-of-the-sahara.html/

• 'Living Machines' use natural, microbial ecosystems to replace industrial sewage and water treatment systems in industry and urban areas (Todd & Todd, 1994). In a Chinese village, for example, a natural ecosystem integrated with a floating walkway, converted a 600 meter raw sewage canal into 750,000 gallons of treated domestic water daily. http://www.oceanarksint.org/

• 'Hedonistic architecture' is represented by a power plant combined with a ski slope and green walls (Bjarke Ingels Group, Denmark). http://inhabitat.com/work-begins-on-bigs-waste-to-energy-ski-slope-project-in-copenhagen/

• 'Playgardens' combine landscapes and eco-service functions with community building environments (Birkeland, 1994). Play equipment has also been used to operate water pumps in African villages. http://www.newsolarpump.com/comparison/hand-water-pump/hand-pump-monolift-playground-pumps.html

• 'Aquaponics' is a closed loop system that could be net positive. Fish waste in a tank produces nutrient-rich water for growing plants. This effluent is converted by microbes into plant food. Plants purify the water making it safe for the fish or aquatic animals in the (fresh or salt) water system. In indoor areas, Light Emitting Diodes can convert solar power collectors into low-cost energy for aquariums. http://aquaponicsjournal.com/

• 'Solar ponds' are salt pools that collect and store solar energy. Solar energy (heat) is trapped in the bottom of a 2 or 3-metre-deep salt pond, as the water is denser than at the surface due to the concentration of salt. The heated water is too heavy to rise and dissipate. At over 90 degrees Celsius the water can be used for process or space heating, or electricity production, and reclaim salinated land in this process http://en.wikipedia.org/wiki/Solar_pond/

• 'Mushrooms' can transform some toxins chemically, such as crude oil, yet the mushrooms remain safe to eat. Non-toxic insecticides from mushrooms can replace harmful agricultural and domestic poisons, restore ecologically damaged habitats, filter water, breakdown toxic waste, and temporarily stabilise eroded forest roads and regenerate forests (Stamets, 2005). http://www.fungi.com/

Box 5 Centre design concept for Australian National Sustainability Initiative (ANSI)

• Green space walls support natural systems that provide environmental and building services, and protect small animal and plant life in terrariums that double as walls.

• Modular walls include some ceiling height gabions containing small rocks to collect and store solar heat in winter, and circulate it throughout the building.

• The structural system is modular and can be constructed off site to gain the savings of prefabricated constructions, and can be expandable or demountable over time.

• Internal atriums provide thermal functions and collect or ventilate warmth and coolness (as do roof greenhouses), and also create internal garden-like work spaces.

• A suspended walkway through an indigenous bird, mammal, insect and reptile species terrarium helps to integrate indoor and outdoor living with visual amenity.

• Ventilated eco-modules have different kinds of exterior screens controlled by interior sensors that roll down as needed, including a storm curtain.

• Modules face a whole gamut of directions and are individually climate controlled to show that, while they should face the sun, one can solar heat buildings in any orientation.

• Modules containing ecosystems will be managed by the local herpetology and entomology societies and/or other community groups, while providing 'living wallpaper'.

• The structure respects the soil. It is off the ground (with under-floor insulation). It uses vertical thermal mass for heating and cooling, which is provided in certain walls.

• The structure 'floats' on the site above the flood level. The vertical structural trusses that support the space frames do not require concrete footings.

• The open plan, modular design and versatile exterior walls can be easily modified over time to integrate unanticipated changes in technology or society.

Eco-positive design reporting

The eco-positive design reporting (EDR) frontloads design by making proponents explain the design research that has been undertaken to meet the 'Sustainability Standard'. Instead of designing first and measuring negative impacts after, it demands design research and self-education (Birkeland, 1996). Proponents need to explicitly identify the negative impacts and how they are reversed. The EDR is then subject to challenge by assessors and the public, and backed up by a 'public' post occupancy evaluation so designers can learn from, or build upon, other's efforts. On less significant development proposals it can replace impact assessments or, on more significant proposals, it can supplement them).

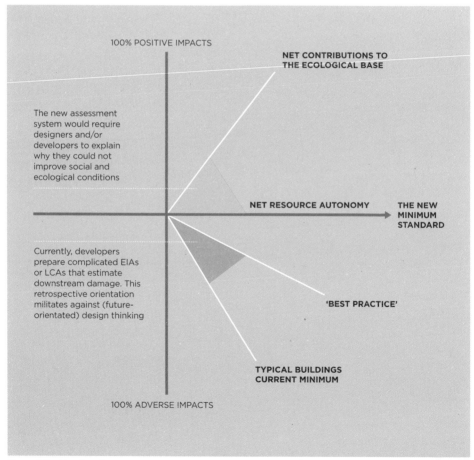

Figure 3 **Positive Development assessment** (Birkeland, 2004)

The starfish below (Figure 4), generated by a spreadsheet program, allows one to visualise total net positive eco-services provided by a design. Each spoke in the 'web' can have a different scale and different units, as only a couple of measurements on each spoke are needed. This can be converted to a single number automatically to compare designs, if necessary. These diagrams are used in life cycle analyses, but they only measure negative impacts, or reductions in negatives compared to a typical building. That is, they score from '-1' (very bad) to '0' (zero harm). In the starfish, net impacts are assessed by placing positive, negative and less negative impacts on the same spectrum in relation to floor area and pre-industrial conditions. The eco-positive 'starfish' diagram keeps negative, regenerative and net positive impacts separate (Birkeland, 2010).

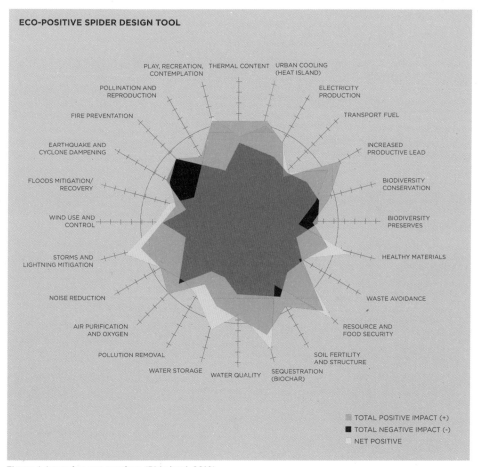

Figure 4 **Assessing eco-services** (Birkeland, 2010)

Eco-positive retrofitting

While important, 'eco-cities' are not a sustainable alternative in themselves. So far, most are commercial business parks and shopping malls that do little to help the poor left in old cities with environmental and economic problems. Even if new cities were designed to include the poor and ecosystems, there is not enough time, money, materials and energy to replace old cities with new green ones. Nor is there enough capacity for nature to absorb the resource extraction and wastes that would be involved. Of course, there will always be a need for new buildings, and there are always materials and wastes entailed in retrofitting as well. Yet to reverse the on-going negative impacts of past design and to increase the life support system, existing cities must be retrofitted.

Eco-positive retrofitting can begin to counterbalance the accelerating population growth, greenhouse emissions, biodiversity and habitat losses. Needless to say, this must be done with the help of ecologists, hydrologists and other environmental experts, due to the lack of ecological knowledge in the development industries. Eco-positive retrofitting can happen quickly as it can be simultaneous, self-funding and create its own clients. It can also operate with or without government help. For example, planners could create point or credit systems for Ecological Space (in atriums, living walls and roofs, green scaffolding, green space walls, etc.) that provide multiple positive benefits (Box 4). Objections to retrofitting are less likely than in the case of new buildings, as retrofitting can preserve historic building facades while increasing resource autonomy, biodiversity and energy efficiency (Birkeland, 2008, p33). If retrofitting is done within an eco-positive framework, then urban areas could indeed become drivers of sustainability, but this has not been the case. To date, retrofitting has not been done in an eco-positive manner.

Despite the unlimited and positive prospects for business, society and nature, and at least 20 years of advocacy (Heede, 1995), even ordinary 'energy retrofitting' (the low-hanging fruit) has not yet been widely taken up. Few green building organisations have capitalised on eco-retrofitting, partly because they rely on existing firms for support, and many firms lack experience. Eco-retrofitting does not fit into the linear-industrial system's mass production conveyor belt and its supply chains and, of course, passive systems are not proprietary. As no one owns the sun, corporations (the market) largely ignore passive retrofitting opportunities. However, Eco-positive retrofitting can conform to the industrial supply chain, yet change it, through the use of prefabricated, passive multi-functional, retrofit modules that avoid altering the structure and environmental costs of waste. To reduce the costs of site-specific design, basic modules could be factory produced and adapted to each orientation and microclimate.

Passive solar modules can also include solar films and/or photovoltaic cells as well. Existing curtain glass walls, which are even found on so-called 'green' buildings, are inefficient in energy usage and increase the urban heat island effect. However, these could be covered with new transparent films that resist heat gain in summer and heat loss in winter, and/or have embedded photovoltaic cells for electricity production. Parts of curtain glass facades could be covered by pollution absorbing filters and sound-absorbing materials as well, or even planting modules where accessible for maintenance. In some cases, these modules can also use the 'free' services of fungi, bacteria, algae, plants and invertebrates like worms to turn 'waste' into clean energy, air, water, soil and/or food as in Green Scaffolding (see Birkeland, 2013b). Modules across all scales and levels of urban structures for small business or 'do-it-yourself' homeowners are available.

Box 6 **Benefits of eco-retrofitting**

Eco-retrofitting is better than doing nothing, because it makes owners, occupants and the society as a whole better off and saves resources and money. Eco-positive retrofitting would capitalise on the positives, avoid the negatives, and increase the ecology.

• Worker health and productivity, a major factor in business profits, can be greatly improved by natural lighting, organic materials, air quality, etc. although the exact amount cannot be predicted.

• Renovating for energy efficiency alone can pay for itself. Retrofitting for passive solar design can eliminate much of the operating energy of existing buildings. Green products can significantly reduce the electricity used by office equipment.

• Retrofitting usually costs less than a new building, as using the old structure can save about a third of costs and materials. Buildings need upgrading and renovations regularly so eco-retrofitting should be seen as the cost of doing business, not an extra.

• Like many other products, new building components are often designed for planned obsolescence and building interiors are gutted for new clients on a regular basis or facades get exterior 'face lifts' to attract higher rents.

• 'Tried and true' systems, such as 'performance contracting' can cover the upfront costs of retrofits (AEPCA, 2007). The contractor's costs and profits are recovered from the energy savings so the client pays nothing and eventually inherits a reduced energy bill. Many established energy contracting companies already retrofit buildings at no cost to the building owner (although some charge for the preparation of quotes).

• Retrofitting is an investment. One can buy securities in retrofitting which compare favourably with stock and bonds (Romm, 1999).

• The savings from 'energy retrofitting' can be rolled-over in areas where further resource savings are possible, but which are less lucrative. Otherwise, energy service contractors can pick the low hanging fruit and leave.

• In some regions, the material flows in conventional renovations exceed that of new construction and toxic materials are land-filled, only to be replaced by other toxic materials. It is often better to encapsulate asbestos and other toxins.

• Eco-retrofitting could increase net eco-services and natural security (eg. food, water, air, absorb CO_2), without disrupting occupants, so the building can continue to pay rent.

Mapping ethical business opportunities

Where would PD start? PD is essentially the opposite of DP and begins from a different starting point: critique. As shown in Figure 5, identifying negatives helps to identify places where eco-positive design can be most effective, and perhaps pay for itself in a whole systems framework. Systems Mapping and Redesign Thinking (SMARTmode) is a set of PD processes, methods and forensic audits to identify information needed for eco-positive planning and design. This information is largely absent in government as statistical data was gathered for purposes of business and industrial growth, not human and ecological health (Norton, 2005). SMARTmode is intended to expose and correct many of the fundamental biases against sustainability that are embedded in contemporary environmental management methods and tools (see Birkeland, 2013b). SMARTmode Analyses make the linear flows in the current approach to development transparent:

• from public to private interests, causing a loss of future democratic control;
• from the poor to the wealthy, causing a loss of individual self-determination;
• from the lay public to experts, causing a loss of cross-disciplinarity and lack of critique;
• from the future to present generations, causing a loss of future social choice and adaptive capacity;
• from the environment to development, causing a loss of natural capital and ecosystem resilience.

Visualisation and communication

The complexity of sustainability-relevant data can be managed by new visualisation technologies. These have the potential to combine sustainability investment decision making with powerful new information management systems (Jackson & Simpson, 2012). These digital technologies could enable meaningful community engagement and transparency in urban decision making. This would put local citizens and international experts on the same page to improve public debate, facilitate problem solving and envision better futures. If the emerging information and visualisation technologies are integrated into a Positive Development framework, environmental agencies and citizens would be empowered to:

• integrate heretofore missing sustainability information into all levels of urban development, planning and design;
• identify eco-positive business opportunities that could create healthier cities and citizens;
• deal with the complex issues involved in intervening in existing cities to increase biophysical and social sustainability;
• visually explore development scenarios on many levels;
• identify areas for priority investments in green infrastructure and eco-logical retrofitting;
• prioritise structures needing future proofing for earthquakes, floods, volcanoes, droughts, cyclones, etc;
• map equity, risk and health issues for preventative action, not procrastination.

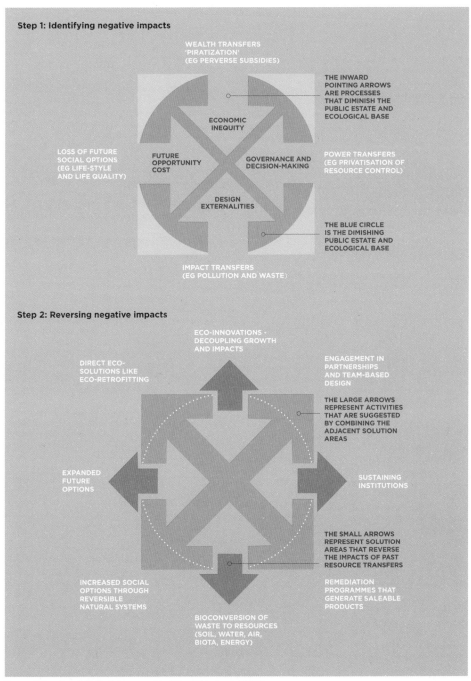

Step 1: Identifying negative impacts

WEALTH TRANSFERS 'PIRATIZATION' (EG PERVERSE SUBSIDIES)

THE INWARD POINTING ARROWS ARE PROCESSES THAT DIMINISH THE PUBLIC ESTATE AND ECOLOGICAL BASE

ECONOMIC INEQUITY

LOSS OF FUTURE SOCIAL OPTIONS (EG LIFE-STYLE AND LIFE QUALITY)

FUTURE OPPORTUNITY COST

GOVERNANCE AND DECISION-MAKING

POWER TRANSFERS (EG PRIVATISATION OF RESOURCE CONTROL)

DESIGN EXTERNALITIES

THE BLUE CIRCLE IS THE DIMISHING PUBLIC ESTATE AND ECOLOGICAL BASE

IMPACT TRANSFERS (EG POLLUTION AND WASTE)

Step 2: Reversing negative impacts

ECO-INNOVATIONS - DECOUPLING GROWTH AND IMPACTS

DIRECT ECO-SOLUTIONS LIKE ECO-RETROFITTING

ENGAGEMENT IN PARTNERSHIPS AND TEAM-BASED DESIGN

THE LARGE ARROWS REPRESENT ACTIVITIES THAT ARE SUGGESTED BY COMBINING THE ADJACENT SOLUTION AREAS

EXPANDED FUTURE OPTIONS

SUSTAINING INSTITUTIONS

THE SMALL ARROWS REPRESENT SOLUTION AREAS THAT REVERSE THE IMPACTS OF PAST RESOURCE TRANSFERS

INCREASED SOCIAL OPTIONS THROUGH REVERSIBLE NATURAL SYSTEMS

REMEDIATION PROGRAMMES THAT GENERATE SALEABLE PRODUCTS

BIOCONVERSION OF WASTE TO RESOURCES (SOIL, WATER, AIR, BIOTA, ENERGY)

Figure 5 **Turning deficits into opportunities** (Birkeland, 2008)

In summary, given a shrinking world, development must, at the very least, increase the ecological base, equitable living conditions and future social choice. There are unprecedented grounds for optimism if urban development is reconceived as a sustainability solution. To do so requires a positive paradigm that places ecology, design and ethics in a central place in decision making and design. Although linear industrial progress has absolute limits, and these have been irreversibly breached, living conditions for everyone could be greatly improved with PD. There are no limits to perpetual improvement in economic, social and environmental quality through eco-positive systems design. However, eternal vigilance is required to ensure that emerging design, decision and visualisation frameworks are mobilised in the public interest, and not re-colonised by the ruling paradigm of (industrial) sustainable development.

References

AEPCA (2007) The Australasian Energy Performance Contracting Association http://www.eec.org.au/

AIA Research Corporation (1976) *Solar Dwelling Design Concepts,* US Department of Housing and Urban Development, Washington, DC

Ayres, R.U. and U.E. Simonis (eds) (1994) *Industrial Metabolism: Restructuring for Sustainable Development,* UN University Press: Tokyo, NY

Beattie, A. and P. Ehrlich (2004) *Wild Solutions* (second edition), Yale University Press: New Haven, CT

Birkeland, J.L. (2002) *Design for Sustainability: A Sourcebook of Integrated Eco-logical Solutions,* Earthscan, London (now Routledge)

Birkeland, J.L. (2004) *Building Assessment Systems: Reversing Environmental Impacts,* website discussion paper, Nature and Society Forum, Canberra, ACT

Birkeland, J.L. (2009a) *Design for eco-services. Part A – Environmental Services, Environment Design Guide (77)* (Canberra, Architects Institute of Australia) p1-13 http://www.environmentdesignguide.com.au/

Birkeland, J.L. (2009b) *Design for eco-services. Part B – Building Services, Environmental Design Guide (78)* (Canberra, Architects Institute of Australia) p1-9

Birkeland, J.L. (1994) 'Ecofeminist Playgardens', *International Play Journal* 2, p49-59

Birkeland, J.L. (2008) *Positive Development: From Vicious Circles to Virtuous Cycles through Built Environment Design,* London, UK: Earthscan (now Routledge)

Birkeland, J.L. (2010) 'Positive Communities', DEEDI (Queensland Government) Workshop, September 23, Brisbane, Queensland

Birkeland, J.L. (2013a) 'Positive Development', in Byrne, J., Dodson J., & Sipe, N. (eds) *Australian Environmental Planning: Challenges and Future Prospects,* London: Routledge

Birkeland, J.L. (2013b) 'Sustainable Resilient Buildings' book chapter for L. Pearson, P. Newton and P. Roberts (Eds) *Resilient Sustainable Cities,* Routledge, UK

Boyden, S., S. Millar, K. Newcombe and B. O'Neill (1981) *The Ecology of a City and its People: The Case of Hong Kong,* Australian National University Press, Canberra

BRI, Building Research and Information (2012) 40 (1) (a whole edition on regenerative design), http://www.tandfonline.com/loi/rbri20

Corbett, J. and M. Corbett (1999) 'Toward better neighbourhood design', College of Human Ecology, Michigan State University, http://www.lgc.org/freepub/community_design/articles/energy_better_design/index.html

Crawford, R. and G. Treloar (2005) 'An assessment of the energy and water embodied in commercial building construction', paper presented at Fourth Australian LCA Conference, Sydney, Australia

CSIRO (1998) 'Smart buildings to deliver huge savings', media release, ref 98/48, 5 March

Daily, G. and K. Ellison (2002) *The New Economy of Nature,* Island Press, Washington, DC

Esty, D.C. and A.S. Wilston (2006) *Green to Gold: How Smart Companies Use Environmental Strategy to Innovate, Create Value and Build Competitive Advantage,* Yale University Press, New Haven, CT, and London

Edwards, B. (1998) *Green Buildings Pay,* Spon Press, London

Folke, C. Jansson, Å., Larsson, J. & Costanza, R. (1997) 'Ecosystem Appropriation by Cities, Ambio Vol 26, p167-172

GBCA (2006) *The Dollars and Sense of Green Buildings: Building the Business Case for Green Commercial Buildings in Australia,* GBCA, Sydney, Australia

Gillespie, G. (2008) 'Organic Waste to Farms' in Birkeland, J. (ed.) *Positive Development: From Vicious Circles to Virtuous Cycle through Built Environment Design* (Earthscan, London)

Hamilton, C. (1994) *The Mystic Economist, Willow* Park Press, Canberra, Australia

Hargroves, C. and M.H. Smith (2005) *The Natural Advantage of Nations,* Earthscan, London

Harrison, D., A.M. Chalkley and E. Billet (2002) 'The rebound effect', in J. Birkeland (ed) *Design for Sustainability: A Sourcebook of Integrated Eco-logical Solutions,* Earthscan, London, p129

Hawken, P. (1993) *The Ecology of Commerce: a declaration of sustainability,* HarperBusiness: New York

Hawken, P., A. Lovins and H. Lovins (1999) *Natural Capitalism: Creating the Next Industrial Revolution,* Earthscan, London

Heal, G. (2000) *Nature and the Marketplace: Capturing the Value of Ecosystem Services,* Island Press: Washington, DC

Heede, R. et al (1995) *Homemade Money,* Rocky Mountain Institute with Brick House Publishing, Harrisville, NH

Hill, G. (2002) 'Designing waste', in J. Birkeland (ed) *Design for Sustainability: A Sourcebook of Integrated Eco-logical Solutions,* Earthscan, London, p43-45

HM Treasury (2006) *Stern Review: The Economics of Climate Change,* UK Government, London, downloadable from http://webarchive.nationalarchives.gov.uk/+/http:/www.hm-treasury.gov.uk/sternreview_index.htm

IUCN/UNEP/WWF (1980) 'World Conservation Strategy', re-published in 1991 as *Caring for the Earth: A Strategy for Sustainable Living,* IUCN (The World Conservation Union)/UNEP (United Nations Environment Programme)/WWF (World Wide Fund for Nature), London: Earthscan

Jackson, D. & Simpson, R., eds. (2012) *D_City: Digital Earth, Virtual Nations,* Data Cities, DCity: Sydney, Australia

Johnson, R. (1979) *The Green City,* MacMillan: S. Melbourne, Australia

Kats, G. (2003) *The Costs and Financial Benefits of Green Buildings: A Report to California's Sustainable Building Task Force,* CSBTF, San Francisco, CA

Kok N. (2009) 'Doing Well by Doing Good: Green Office Buildings', Profitable Sustainability in Property, Conference of the Australian Property Institute, Sydney. http://www.adpia.com.au/

Larsson, M. (2008) Dune, Thesis at the Architectural Association, London, see http://news.bbc.co.uk/1/hi/technology/8166929.stm. Accessed September 2011

LBC, Living Building Challenge (2010) A Visionary Path to a Restorative Future. International Living Building Institute, Seattle, Washington, USA. http://living-future.org/lbc

Lyle, J.T. (1994) Regenerative Design for Sustainable Development, Wiley & Sons: New York

Marmot, M. (2004) *Status Syndrome: How Your Social Standing Directly Affects Your Health and Life Expectancy,* Bloomsbury and Henry Holt, New York

McDonough, W. and M. Braungart (2002) *Cradle to Cradle: Remaking the Way we Make Things,* North Point Press, New York

McLennan, J. F. (2004) *The Philosophy of Sustainable Design,* Ecotone Publishing, Kansas City, MO

Myers, N. and J. Kent (2001) *Perverse Subsidies: How Tax Dollars Can Undercut the Environment and the Economy,* Island Press, Washington, DC

Norton, B.G. (2005) *Sustainability: A Philosophy of Adaptive Ecosystem Management,* University of Chicago, Press, Chicago, IL

Papanek, V. (1971) Design for the real world: human ecology and social change, Pantheon Books: New York

Renger, C. Birkeland, J.L. and Midmore, D. (2013) *Positive Development: Design for Climate Mitigation and Ecological Gains,* 'SB13 – Vancouver', CA

Repetto, R.C. and M. Gillis (1988) *Public Policies and the Misuse of Forest Resources,* Cambridge University Press: Cambridge, UK

Romm, J. (1999) *Cool Companies: How the Best Businesses Boost Profits and Productivity by Cutting Greenhouse-Gas Emissions,* Island Press, Washington, DC

Rudofsky, B. (1987, first published 1964), *Architecture without Architects,* University of New Mexico Press: Santa Fee, New Mexico

Safamanesh, B., & Byrd, H. (2012) The Two sides of a Double-skin Facade: Built Intelligent Skin or Brand Image Scam. *Proceedings of the 46th Architectural Science Association conference,* NSW, Australia Griffith University

Shurcliff, W.A. (c. 1979) *Solar Heated Buildings of North America: 120 Outstanding Examples,* Brick House Publishing, Harrisville, NH

Schmidt, M. (2010) Ecological design for climate mitigation in contemporary urban living, International Journal of Water, 5(4), p337-352

Stahel, W. (2013) The business angle of a circular economy – higher competitiveness, higher resource security and material efficiency. In: *A New Dynamic - effective business in a circular economy,* EMF 2013 (in press)

Stamets, P. (2005) *Mycelium Running: How Mushrooms Can Help Save the World,* Ten Speed Press, Berkeley, CA

Swain, I. (2008) 'Linking policies to outcomes', in Birkeland, J. (ed.) *Positive Development: From Vicious Circles to Virtuous Cycle through Built Environment Design* (Earthscan, London), p325

Tibbs, H. (2002) 'Industrial ecology' in J. Birkeland (ed) *Design for Sustainability: A Sourcebook of Integrated Ecological Solutions,* Earthscan, London, p52-56

Todd, N.J. and J. Todd (1994) From *Eco-Cities to Living Machines,* N. Atlantic Books, Berkeley, CA

UNEP (2012) *Resilient People, Resilient Planet, A Future Worth Choosing: The UN Secretary General's High-Level Panel on Global Sustainability,* launched 10 January 2012 (www.un.org/gsp/). Accessed April 2012

UN-HABITAT (2011) *Cities and Climate Change: Global Report on Human Settlements.* http://www.unhabitat.org/downloads/docs/GRHS2011_Full.pdf

Vale, B. and R. Vale (1975) *The Autonomous House: Design and Planning* for self-sufficiency, Thames and Hudson Ltd, London, UK

Wann, D. (1996) *Deep Design: Pathways to a Liveable Future,* Island Press, Washington, DC

Wackernagel, M. and W.E. Rees (1996) *Our Ecological Footprint: Reducing the Human Impact on the Earth,* New Society Publishers, Gabriola Island, BC, Canada, and New Haven, CT

Waring, M. (1998) *Counting for Nothing: What Men Value and What Women are Worth,* Bridget Williams Books, Wellington, New Zealand

Weizsacker, E. van, A. Lovins and H. Lovins (1997) Factor 4: *Doubling Wealth – Halving Resource Use,* Earthscan, London

Wilson, E.O. (1993) The Biophilia Hypothesis, S. Kellert, ed. (Island Press, Washington DC)

Wolman, A. (1965) 'The Metabolism of Cities', in *Scientific American,* Vol. 213, no.3, p179-190

Yale Centre for Business and the Environment (2012) http://cbey.yale.edu/

REBUILDING ECONOMIC VITALITY
REV® THE WORLD

8

Sally Goerner and Randolph Voller

We face systemic problems - economic, political, social and environmental ones all wound up together. Effective solutions are emerging in all of these domains, but we lack a sound systemic framework to weave them together. Now, however, the laws of energy networks and keen observations of what does and does not work in human networks are uniting in a common vision of how to build lasting economic vitality. This is the story of how this framework: helps us rediscover the value of free-enterprise democracy; clarifies the human factors that make Democratic Free Enterprise Networks (DFENs) the innovative powerhouses we know they can be; provides quantitative measures for healthy development to guide our steps.

Sally Goerner is director of Triangle Centre for the Study of Complex Systems and president of Integral Science Institute. She is one of the leaders of the international movement to integrate the findings of 'intricacy' research and apply them to human systems from economics to urban planning.

sgoerner@mindspring.com

Randolph Voller is the Mayor of Pittsboro, North Carolina (USA) and a principal of VRC Limited, a business consulting and real estate development firm. His primary interest is in effectively combining economic development, renewable energy, affordable housing and local financing.

Integral Science Institute
www.integralscienceinstitute.org/about_ISI.html

Inspired by insights from living systems, natural capitalists and circular economists such as Braungart and McDonough (2002) have brought a new vision to business using triple-top-line approaches that value human capital, see small as beautiful and support environmental health by cradle to cradle methods such as turning waste into resources and shifting to clean renewable energy.

Unfortunately, linear thinking still dominates, and today's global economic malaise, rising public anxiety and ensuing polarisation seems to be making it worse. People afraid for their livelihoods care more about jobs than environment, and they're apt to vote for those who promise the fastest and most familiar cure – regardless of whether that method actually works. So, paradoxically, in the name of creating jobs by reducing taxes and deficits, we now have austerity measures that eliminate jobs by slashing education, roads, hospitals and police.

How could free markets work differently? We believe the best way to stop today's destructive rush and fully realise the new vision is to repair the free enterprise narrative by creating a more empirically precise and persuasive explanation of what really does create lasting social and economic vitality. Today, for example, we know a lot about the specific causes of the derivative bubble that nearly crashed the global economy in 2008, but the Free Market theories that dominate today lack both a technical explanation for the systemic causes of the crash, and a compelling human narrative of how to restore vitality. Recent expansions to our understanding of everyday energy laws help us address both of these issues.

This chapter uses the science of energy networks, to: 1) clarify the conditions for lasting vitality in economic networks; and 2) provide a clear, empirical framework for the new vision; which, 3) confirms long-standing observations and narratives about how human networks work from such notables as Jane Jacobs, Elinor Ostrom and EF Schumacher. Found under different names around the world from the ancient Greek Paideia to northern Italy's flexible manufacturing networks and Spain's Mondragon cooperatives, we will give the target networks a modern title: Democratic Free Enterprise Networks (DFENs). Instead of blaming intractable human defects such as greed and corruption, energy network laws pin today's crisis on two very tractable traditions:

• Neglecting real-economy networks built of real human beings (DFENs) as the root source of economic vitality, in favour of exaggerated faith in monetary growth (GDP);
• A gross misunderstanding of the social, economic, material and cultural conditions needed to support network vitality.

Creating economic vitality, money versus networks

"... the GDP not only masks the breakdown of the social structure and the natural habitat upon which the economy — and life itself — ultimately depend; worse, it actually portrays such breakdown as economic gain."
Clifford Cobb et al *If the Economy is Up, Why Do You Feel So Down?* 1995

How do you create economic vitality? Most economists would say the main goal is to increase GDP, that is, to increase the volume of money exchanged in the economy. Beyond this, neoliberal theorists would recommend deregulation, privatisation, reducing taxes (particularly on the supply side), rolling back labour and environmental protections, and vigorously pursuing all other such 'structural adjustments'. If the national debt is high, such theorists would also recommend austerity: cutting government spending on people, pensions and services.

These particular beliefs about how to create economic health have dominated first Western and now global economic policy for over 30 years. Though GDP has grown through most of this time, other indicators give one pause, including jobless growth, the erosion of the middle class, the outsourcing of productive capacity to low wage locations around the world, and increasing concentration of wealth and power in the hands of a very few individuals. Figure 1 shows neoliberalism's impact on American worker wages. Figure 2 shows neoliberalism's impact on the global real economy, that is, on the business networks that produce real goods and services. GDP growth masks these situations because it ignores both the cause of monetary growth (speculation vs. real) and where the money goes.

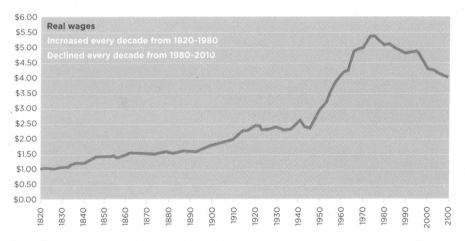

Figure 1 **Average Worker Wages in America 1820-2010 (inflation adjusted)**
Note that each generation was better off than the last for America's first 150 years.

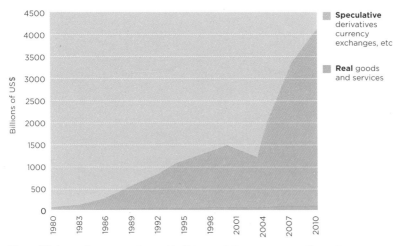

Figure 2 **Volume of money exchanged in the speculative economy vs. the real economy**
Daily volume of foreign exchange transactions as reported by the Bank for International Settlements (BSI) in April each year versus foreign-exchange transactions based on 'real' economic exchanges (1980-2010). The temporary dip in 2004 was due to the replacement of 12 European currencies with the euro. (Revised from Lietaer, et al, 2012)

It is time for a change. Thanks to the global economic crisis begun in 2007, a massive rethinking of capitalism has already begun. This chapter uses everyday energy laws to argue that the problem lies not with free enterprise or even capitalism per se, but with a corruption of these that steadfastly ignores the health of the human networks, which are the real basis of all social and economic health and well-being. The resulting empirical framework confirms empirical observations of what makes human networks thrive, while allowing us to reclaim Free Enterprise's original human narrative, now linking it inseparably to democracy.

Most modern people think about energy in terms of the energy we consume – fossil fuels, electricity, etc. – but physicists think in more universal terms. Here, the very fabric of the universe consists of a dynamic web of forces and flows, where 'forces' refers to gravity, electromagnetism etc., and 'flows' means the flow of energy and, with it, matter and information.

In this view, energy is literally the stuff of which everything is made, including matter itself. Ecosystems and the carbon cycle are both energy flow networks. Metabolism is the name we give to our body's energy processing system. Global climate change is about disrupting existing patterns of flow by turning up the heat. Even 'information' is now thought to be a response to patterned energy trails such as the chemical gradient we call smell or the photon flow we call light.

More recent discoveries suggest that, instead of a seething disorganised mass, our dancing cosmic energy web is actually filled with intricate geometric order, from the curve of atomic decay and a hurricane's organised swirl to the structure of smart growth in cities. This order fits the contemporary concept of fractals, and systems science's original thesis that all systems follow certain universal patterns and principles. (See Figure 3.)

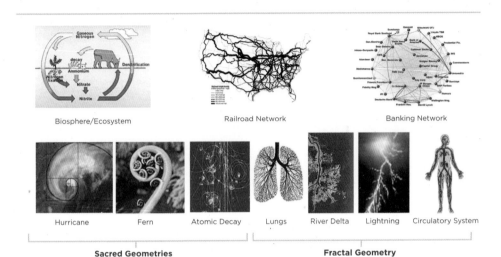

Biosphere/Ecosystem   Railroad Network   Banking Network

Hurricane   Fern   Atomic Decay   Lungs   River Delta   Lightning   Circulatory System

Sacred Geometries   **Fractal Geometry**

Figure 3 **Some energy flow systems and their patterns**

Ilya Prigogine's Nobel-Prize winning work in self-organising systems took this orderly vision to a new level. Here, energy pressures and flow are seen as the driving force behind all growth, development and evolution, literally from the origins of matter and life to the latest cycles of civilisations (Chaisson, 2001; Odum, 2007). In this view, energy pressures and flows form a cosmic self-organising/ordering process that uses recurrent patterns and principles to build the world as we know it. Matter was fused in the high-pressure explosion of the Big Bang. Life was forged in the fiery furnace of early Earth, along with the chemical cycles that still span the globe. Civilisations rise and fall through the seething pressures of information, environment, money and power. This last may seem far-fetched, but, as we show below, there is empirical evidence that societies too follow energy laws.

Newer fields such as nonlinear dynamics (Chaos Theory) and energy network analysis provided the final touches: mathematical clarity and quantitative measures. Instead of general patterns, we now have a remarkably rigorous understanding of the universal patterns and principles of growth, development and evolution that apply to all systems, including living organisms, weather systems, city systems, ocean currents and economies. Ecologists, for example, can now assess ecosystem health/sustainability quantitatively by measuring a network's flow volumes and structural stability (Figure 4). Similarly, fractal network findings have been successfully applied to the operation of cities (Salingaros, 2003) and the oscillating behaviour of stock markets (Peters, 1994).

And, ironically, while ecologists are most famous for modeling ecosystems as energy-flow networks – food chains and the carbon cycle, for instance – the first person to apply energy models to orderly complex systems was Russian economist, Wassily Leontief in the 1950s[1].

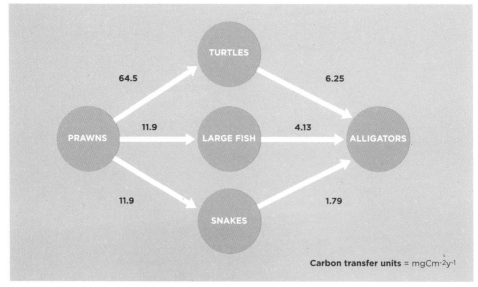

Figure 4 **Measuring network health as a function of structure and circulation**
Ecologists measure structure by counting the number, diversity and size (capacity) of all member components, in this case, alligators, fish, etc. They measure circulation as the volume of chemical flows: carbon, nitrogen, etc. The above chart shows carbon transfer in the cypress wetland ecosystem of southern Florida (after Ulanowicz, et al., 1996).

Instead of imagining the economy heading automatically towards equilibrium, scientists who study energy-driven self-organisation think of economies in terms of pressure that drives cycles of change, diversity that seeds new patterns, and the question of collapse versus the emergence of healthy new organisations and networks. Pressure builds when too many people have too many unmet needs or perceive too much inequity with other members of the society. Unaddressed pressures that 'the powers that be' may attempt to circumvent in the short term, will inevitably come back to haunt in the long term. Self-organisation theory says that, eventually, some naturally occurring 'diversity' – perhaps a compelling narrative or a confirming scientific discovery – will turn long simmering pressure into relatively abrupt change. The only question is whether this change will bring a healthier stage of development or a snowballing roll towards collapse. On the cusp of great change there is hope, but no guarantees. (See Figure 5.)

If you ask this new breed of energy scientists how to create economic vitality, their answers will tend to focus on circulation and network structure. These features are central to system health because they constitute the network's form and function, that is, the goal and means for processing and exchange. And, just as form and function are inseparable, so circulation and structure are also entangled such that problems in one cause problems in the other.

Network structure can be understood using the concepts of economic infrastructure and human capital. If you want your local economic network to avoid becoming a house of cards, you will need to keep your human and economic infrastructure robust

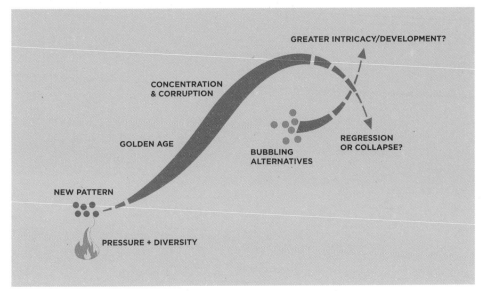

Figure 5 **The standard cycle of civilisation as pressure-driven**

and resilient. This means, among other things, that you'll need good roads, bridges, internet access, phone service, schools, hospitals, banking and investment services. You need robust and resilient structure in all these domains because, if the only bridge into town collapses or the only bank has gone out of business, then your local businesses will produce poorly and many are likely to fail. Network structure's crucial role in economic health can be seen in the powerful benefits of investment programmes such as the Marshall Plan, excellent public schools, high-speed rail, etc.

For the most part, the energy view of economic circulation follows the equilibrium concepts of supply, demand and distribution. Businesses (supply) take in raw materials and produce goods and services, which they then 'circulate' to other stakeholders in the circuit including customers, employees, other businesses and government. Money circulates best when businesses pay salaries, pay taxes, invest in their productive capacity, and buy goods from other businesses. Workers, consumers, businesses and even governments complete the circuit by using the money they receive from employment, purchases and taxes to purchase goods and services.

In an energy view, however, Adam Smith's butcher and baker are not alone in their processing and exchange, but part of a vast interconnected circuit. Like organisms in an ecosystem or cells in your body, every agent in an economy depends on the value-add efforts of others and on maintaining robust on-going flow. Here contribution counts, but so too does quality, honesty and otherwise serving the health of the whole system as well as oneself. Consequently, instead of an exaggerated focus on self-interest, here fitness is defined as, "the ability to play a coherent role in the web of processes" (Ulanowicz, 1986).

This common-cause vision makes certain core beliefs from Right and Left seem much less oppositional. The importance of value-add contribution, for example, confirms the conservative position that contribution counts and free-riders are a problem (see also Elinor Ostrom's work). Yet, confirming that all levels count and that nourishment must reach every member also confirms the progressive view of the importance of commonwealth infrastructure, now expanded from roads and bridges to schools, the media, utilities and banks.

This expanded 'it takes a village' view also explains why 'where money goes' matters. So, unlike neoliberal theories that emphasise maximum profits for owners only, in an energy view all parts of the circuit count and the key to vitality lies in rapid, robust, thorough circulation of money, goods, services etc. to all stakeholders. Furthermore, while money is an essential flow, so too are other commonwealth needs such as accurate information, empowering education, accessible energy, clean water and trained people. Should any of these flows be restricted, then the health of the whole will be harmed. Here, of course, lower wages and closed factories diminish circulation by reducing purchasing power, and Keynesian stimuli are attempts to improve circulation. Yet, circulation and economic health are also diminished by regressive taxation, externalising costs, usury, and businesses that pay little in taxes or sit on billions in profits they are reluctant to invest.

A key corollary is that excessive concentration at the top will tend to cause erosion of lower level networks due to poor circulation. A banking case from my home state illustrates how this works. Bob Wilkinson[2] was a prosperous, North Carolina builder for 35 years... until the money for small-scale development loans dried up in 2008. The problem wasn't that Bob didn't have collateral or wasn't paying his bills or didn't have a great track record. No, the problem was that the local bank Bob had dealt with for many years had been bought by a bigger bank, which had been bought by a bigger bank still. The new gargantuan bank didn't know who Bob was and didn't care. For them, Bob was too small to be worth the cost of giving him a loan.

Bob and thousands like him are still going out of business because big banks find it too costly to invest in little guys. Unfortunately, a destructive domino effect then follows. When people like Bob go out of business: their employees lose their jobs; their suppliers lose business; the school district loses taxes; and all the businesses that supply food, gas, healthcare, clothing, etc. to all those people lose money as well. As stories like Bob's multiply, local economies become ever more fragile – even as the big banks and corporations accumulate more and more cash that they stash in Cayman Island accounts to avoid paying taxes. The result is withering businesses, bankrupt local governments, crumbling infrastructure and fired teachers.

Thus, a bubble economy is not unstable because there isn't enough money in the system, but because the money is not circulating sufficiently to lower scale producers and consumers. This axiom applies directly to our current economic malaise. There is ample evidence that major corporations around the globe are sitting on billions of poorly circulating profits. Having lost trillions in speculation, major banks and investment houses are also loath to make commercial and housing loans to little guys. Since upper-scale organisations tend to circulate money mostly amongst themselves, reducing taxes on the wealthy leaves even more money stranded in the stratosphere. Instead of nourishing commonwealth infrastructure for all, elite money trickles down poorly and incompletely.

Austerity programmes make matters worse – think Greece. Austerity measures undermine circulation and economic health by slashing the wages, benefits, roads, schools, police and healthcare that support the country's commonwealth infrastructure, while keeping the interest payments to banks and payouts to big corporations that siphon money away from the same.

Unfortunately, since economic systems seem structured to drain wealth from the real economy and concentrate it at the top, it is hard to imagine how else Free Enterprise Networks could work. Luckily, nature provides an answer in its design of two particularly powerful circulation structures, fractals and intricacy.

The structure of vitality

"It's not how big you grow; it's how you grow big."
Jane Jacobs *Ideas that Matter conference,* 1997

Theory and observation suggest that the only networks that last are ones that maintain: 1) rapid, robust, thorough circulation to all parts of the whole; and 2) structural stability, that is, ones that avoid becoming unstable like a house of cards. Fractals and intricacy abound in the real world because they address both of these needs. Their design teaches us a lot about the real causes of vitality (and lack thereof) in human systems. Their structure and flow characteristics also allow us to define and measure 'healthy development' quantitatively. Such measures help transform Jane Jacobs' keen observations and compelling narrative of human networks into the kind of mathematical precision, which economists so often demand.

Intricacy: Small & Connected = Strength & Speed

"Cities ... need all kinds of diversity, intricately mingled in mutual support. They need this so city life can work decently and constructively, and so the people of cities can sustain ... their society and civilisation. ... I think that the science of city planning ... must become the science and art of catalysing and nourishing diverse, close-grained working relationships that support each other economically and socially."
Jane Jacobs *Cities and the Wealth of Nations,* 1961

Jane Jacobs, who penned the opening quote over 50 years ago, was applying the then new concept of ordered complexity to her observations of what makes cities work. Intricacy provides an empirical explanation of what she was saying.

Intricacy refers to the lace like network of small, interconnected, synergetic circles that nature uses to weave smaller pieces into ever bigger wholes. Molecules are built of atoms which are built of subatomic particles. Your body is built of organs and tissues that are built of individual cells. Armies are built of divisions, regiments, brigades and platoons. Intricacy abounds because it enhances circulation, resilience and structural stability at the lower levels of an economic system and at the core of any large organisation. (See Figure 6.)

Reminiscent of EF Schumacher, intricacy teaches us that, small and connected equals strength and speed. Thus, small, tight teams work better than big bulky ones, but linking small tight teams in a close, synergistic weave works best of all. Because the ties that bind intricate groups must be both strong and flexible, merits such as trust, commitment, quality and integrity all become important to lasting vitality and sustainable economic health.

Since increasing intricacy marks all evolutionary progression, it also teaches us to see new stages of development as new stages of intricacy. (See Figure 7.) A developing embryo shows how intricacy increases. Thus, an embryo starts with a single cell that grows, divides and reconnects with its twin. The process repeats over and over again leading to an intricate network of cells. The energy rule that explains this process gives us new insights into the 'what, why and how's' of healthy growth and development.

As seen in the progression from small groups to large, an organisation may start small, tight, flexible and effective, but as it grows the bonds holding the group together become stretched, while at the same time its bulk makes it less efficient and responsive (the dinosaur effect). If this cohesion-stretching process continues, the organisation will eventually reach a breaking point and a choice point. At this point, it must either: 1) stop growing; 2) find a way to restore small, tight circles and link them synergistically; or 3) face regression and possible collapse.

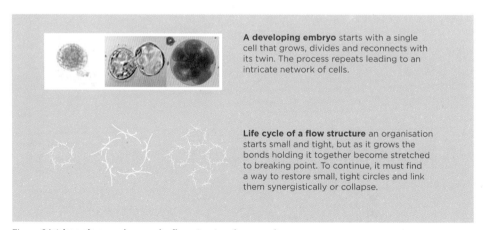

A developing embryo starts with a single cell that grows, divides and reconnects with its twin. The process repeats leading to an intricate network of cells.

Life cycle of a flow structure an organisation starts small and tight, but as it grows the bonds holding it together become stretched to breaking point. To continue, it must find a way to restore small, tight circles and link them synergistically or collapse.

Figure 6 **Intricacy in an embryo and a flow structure in general**
Ever notice that big things are built out of smaller pieces that are built out of smaller pieces still? Energy scientists attribute this pattern to an energy rule called the Surface Volume Law. Seen in how a single cell develops into a multicellular embryo, this rule says that, as a cell grows, the bonds holding it together become stretched until eventually reaching a precise breaking point determined by the ratio of its total volume to its surface area. At this point, the flow structure will either reorganise more intricately or collapse.

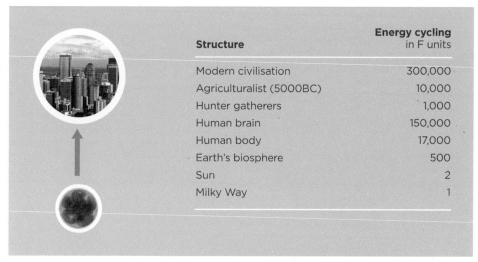

Structure	Energy cycling in F units
Modern civilisation	300,000
Agriculturalist (5000BC)	10,000
Hunter gatherers	1,000
Human brain	150,000
Human body	17,000
Earth's biosphere	500
Sun	2
Milky Way	1

Figure 7 **Increasing intricacy from galaxies to civilisation, measured by energy cycling speed**

Because intricacy's tight weave increases the speed of internal energy circulation, we can measure intricacy using Flux Density (F=ergs/sec -1 gm-1) internal energy cycling speed/ unit time/unit mass. Since energy cycling speed increases in step with stages of development, scientists use Flux Density and intricacy as measures of development.

F=Flux density = energy cycling per unit time/density = ergs per sec-1 gm-1
Eric Chaisson, The Rise of Complexity, *2002*

Human intricacy at work

"It is perfectly possible to imagine a company with an ambitious strategic intent being effortlessly out-performed by what appears to be a disorganized ... network of companies." Tom Lloyd, *Financial Times, 9/8/95*

What does intricacy look like in real life? Ben Cohen, founder of Ben & Jerry's Ice Cream, described business as, "a system of organised human effort that produces power". Intricacy suggests a similar view. Here, healthy business networks are:

"Intricate webs of human expertise, material infrastructure, behavioural patterns, and cultural systems that have grown up together such that all elements play mutually-supportive roles in the well-being of every member of the social, economic and environmental whole." Sally Goerner, *2008*

Found from the industrial cities of Bologna and Venice in northern Italy to Silicon Valley in the US and Asian Motors in Japan, intricate networks exhibit high levels of improvisation and adaptation in design, materials, goods, services and methods of production because such creativity happens best in small firms that are close to the problem and not hampered by bureaucracy or corporate norms. Describing intricacy in the "innumerable small firms in a great cluster of small industrial cities in north-eastern Italy", Charles Sabel emphasizes improvisation as an everyday event:

"A small shop producing tractor transmissions for a large manufacturer modifies the design to suit the need of a small manufacturer of high-quality seeders. In another little shop a conventional automatic packing machine is redesigned to fit the available space in a particular assembly line ... A membrane pump used in automobiles is modified to suit agricultural machinery." Cited in Jacobs, *1984*

Because they are small, cooperative, and inter-linked, such enterprises tend to produce very sophisticated, high-quality work. Innovation is high because improvisation is a central theme. Quality is high because craftsmanship is still important. Craftsmanship is important because human ties still bind. Hence, here people pursue quality and integrity, as well as profit.

Quality and creativity are also high because workers and ideas circulate. Such circulation builds expertise, breadth of experience and an invisible chain of valued human connections. Breakaway enterprises spring up easily and often as workers from older enterprises move out to start firms of their own. Such spin-offs often collaborate with the older establishments because they share history and have related work. People in such networks establish their own 'coherent role in the web of processes', while members, information and expertise cycle easily throughout. Members prosper in a synergetic way (not zero sum) because advances anywhere tend to stimulate benefits everywhere.

Such networks achieve tremendous economies of scale not within the framework of huge organisations as conventionally assumed, but rather through large symbiotic collections of small enterprises. Most have but five to 50 workers with a few more having one or two hundred. As Sabel says:

"The innovative capacity of this type of firm depends on its flexible use of technology; its close relations with other similarly innovative firms in the same and adjacent sectors; and above all on the close collaboration of workers with different kinds of expertise. These firms practice boldly and spontaneously the fusion of conception and execution, abstract and practical knowledge that only a few exceptional giant firms have so far been able to achieve."

Fractals: cross-scale integration and leadership that serves the health of the whole
Fractal structures take this image of synergetic flow to the next level. Seen in the familiar branching structure of your circulatory system (Figure 1) – with a few large conduits (arteries) connecting to successively more numerous and fine-grained smaller conduits (veins to capillaries) – fractal networks provide the efficient cross-scale circulation and unifying core needed to keep large organisations functioning as effective wholes. Also seen in river systems and predator-prey networks, fractals abound in nature because their particular ratio of small, medium and large optimises circulation to all levels. Big, highly efficient conduits (ones with 'economies of scale') support rapid cross-scale circulation, while the more numerous small conduits bring nourishment to every cell. Fractals explain why hierarchy and large-scale players are necessary but not sufficient. To be precise, fractals teach us that vitality requires a balance of:

• *Big & Little,* supporting the more numerous and resilient small-scale businesses and individuals, not just the big, highly efficient players;

• *Flexibility & Constraint,* nourishing innovation, adaptation and learning (flexibility) while restraining activities that harm the whole;

• *Diversity & Community Coherence,* protecting diversity while forging a daily visible, profoundly trusted sense of common-cause across groups.

Where intricacy taught us about the need for small circles and tight weave, fractals teach us about the need for integration, synergy, trust and integrity across scales.
The result is a radically new view of the relationship between top and bottom and of the role of power and leadership in maintaining a healthy whole. Thus, unlike command-and-control hierarchies, fractal networks work best on distributed intelligence and empowerment, with decisions being made at the lowest level possible (subsidiarity). Flexibility and diversity are essential in such systems, but so too are community coherence and constraint from activities that harm the whole. Naturally, in such systems power and leadership aren't about owning and controlling, but about facilitating the long-term health of the whole by coordinating, empowering, and building trust, integrity and common-cause.

The resulting picture mirrors not only employee-owned enterprises and cooperatives such as Mondragon, but also the portrait of extremely long-lived companies described by Arie De Geus in *The Living Company* (2002). As part of a Shell Oil scenario planning project, De Geus was asked to research why some companies, such as Stora in Sweden and Sumitomo in Japan, live for hundreds of years (both of these were founded in the 1200s), while the average lifespan of modern corporations was plummeting and now stood below 20 years. De Geus's findings are stunning. Long-lived companies had a very similar corporate culture, regardless of their country of origin. Perhaps the three biggest keys to longevity appeared to be: 1) valuing people above material equipment; 2) putting the messiness of learning above the orderliness of procedures; and 3) shepherding resources to maintain the long-term health of the whole.

The three balances even provide guidelines for how to get cross-scale synergy and integration to work. For example, where 'divide and conquer' is a great way for elites to maintain temporary control, it is a terrible way to create a healthy society. Where freedom (flexibility) is crucial to learning and adaptation, removing too many constraints from big players in particular leads to monopolistic dominance ('might makes right') that destroys learning and adaptation in the society as a whole. Where we once thought economic health came from maximising profit for owners only, we now realise that vitality only comes from systems that maintain the health and well-being of all stakeholders, not just those at the top.

This view also sheds new light on how various economic policies and political positions help or hinder vitality. Here, for example, antitrust laws, progressive taxation and corporate regulation are important not because great wealth, size, power and efficiency are bad per se, but because too much of any of these will undermine the health of the whole by starving small-scale diversity and resilience[3]. Conversely, policies that nourish human capital and small-scale networks by supporting empowering education, living wages, accessible financing etc. also nourish resilience and, from there, systemic social and economic health.

Furthermore, because fractals follow a mathematically precise (power law) ratio of small, medium and large across scales, we can use nature's system of healthy networks to create precise quantitative measures of healthy development in human networks as well. Ulanowicz, Goerner and Lietaer (Ulanowicz et al, 2009; Goerner et al, 2009), for example, used this concept of precise balance to create a quantitative measure of Sustainable Economic Development (QED) in terms of a balance of resilience (diversity) and efficiency (highly efficient flow). (See Figure 8.)

Last but not least, understanding how growth pressures drive the emergence of more intricate fractal structures also helps us understand why today's command-and-control hierarchies emerged and why global civilisation is due for a fractal shift. In an energy view, social systems are intricate collaborations that need to stay connected, but tend to pull apart as they grow. Villagers in the early agricultural period, for instance, communicated and developed shared understandings easily in the course of constant, close contact. As the population grew, however, this close-weave unravelled. As villages burgeoned into cities, cohesion became harder to maintain.

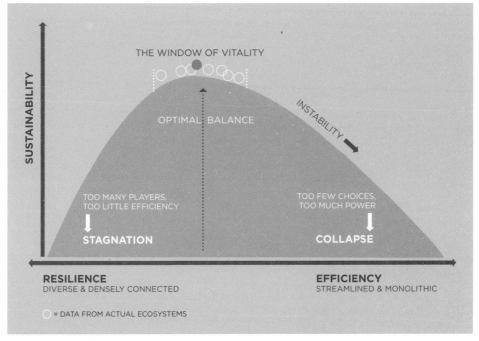

Figure 8 **Measuring economic sustainability as a balance of resilience and efficiency**
The needed balance of big and little is sometimes described as a balance between resilience (densely connected diversity) and efficiency (streamlining/economies of scale). Using data from actual ecosystems, theoretical ecologist Robert Ulanowicz (2009) has shown that 'sustainable' systems maintain a balance of resilience and efficiency that lies within a small range or 'Window of Vitality' around the optimum. Too much efficiency leads to instability and possible collapse due to too few choices and too much power. Too much resilience leads to stagnation due to too many small-scale players and too little efficiency.

Anthropologist Robert Carneiro (1967) believes that the hierarchical social structures we use today were pushed into being by the ensuing growth crisis. He suggests that sprawling, poorly-knit agrarian villages would have been easy prey for marauding tribes envious of their wealth. Unable to coordinate well for defence, many would have simply died out. Others survived by inventing a new means of maintaining coordination: hierarchy. Thus, one man deciding for all and using an efficient system of enforcement allowed societies to mobilise rapidly for defence. Sitting atop a hierarchy with information flowing up from all sides also helped people at the top to build a broader picture, while money flowing to the top allowed them to pay for common-cause infrastructure such as roads and armies. Hence, a king with a bureaucracy serves the same role as a brain and nervous system: they help a large complex collective act as a fast-moving, highly coordinated, far-seeing whole.

So the early command-and-control hierarchies did serve the health of the whole by defence, infrastructure projects, and greater focus, vision and coordination. Unfortunately, as chiefdoms grew into kingdoms and then empires, elites tended to grow apart from their own people. Whatever social contract originally held the powerful in check became more and more fragile. As constraints weakened, exploitation, corruption and concentration of wealth grew, and societal vitality plummeted. If uncorrected, unmet pressures would drive the society into one of three futures: regression; collapse; or a transformative upheaval opening into a progressive reform (such as democracy). The result is the familiar rise and fall of oligarchic civilisations. So, though most modern economists assume today's elite-serving hierarchies are the end pattern of civilisation, fractal theorists would disagree. In their view, command-and-control hierarchies are too rigid to handle the pace of change, and concentrating wealth at the top doesn't leave enough circulation to nourish a vast global civilisation. Only a more fractal network run on servant leadership, democratic constraints on power, and distributed intelligence and empowerment throughout can address these needs. So, though we've been using militaristic hierarchies for 5,000 years, we believe pressure is building for a new fractal evolutionary leap.

Changing our perspective and our dreams

"The gradual development of social equality is at once the past and the future of mankind. To attempt to check democracy would be to attempt to check the will of God." Alexis De Tocqueville, 1835

The energy view provides a firmer economic and social foundation that, ironically, adds new rigour and brings a new positive, practical, achievable focus on people and communities as well. Constantly channeling major flows towards selfish, controlling, short-term ends leads inevitably to societal self-destruction. This is why past oligarchic civilisations collapsed and it seems to be what we are witnessing today.

In an energy view, economic vitality comes from synergetic networks of individuals, communities, businesses and governments engaged in value-add activities that serve the health of the societal whole as part of their own self-interest. We call this system

Democratic Free Enterprise Networks (DFENs) because the ultimate aim of democracy and free enterprise has always been government and economies run by and for all the people. Big and little; diverse and united; flexible as well as restrained: we now understand the characteristics that build vitality in democratic free enterprise societies a bit better.

Neoliberal theory, however, runs against all this. Instead of balance, neoliberals believe vitality springs from gigantic size, lack of constraint, disregard for other stakeholders and the politics of dominance and division not community coherence. The inadequacy of these beliefs have become so glaring that future generations will probably wonder why we held them so long and applied them so widely.

This brings us full circuit. In an energy view, the only way to restore lasting vitality is to rebuild intricate, fractal DFENs. Living examples of human intricacy give us hope as well as concrete examples of how this can be done. Fractal networks indicate how power and leadership can help.

References

Braungart, M. and McDonough, W. (2002) *Cradle to Cradle: Remaking the Way we Make Things.* New York: North Point Press

Carneiro, R. (1967) On the Relationship between Size of Population and Complexity of Social Structure. *Southwestern Journal of Anthropology,* 23, p234-243

Chaisson, E. (2002) *Cosmic Evolution.* New York: Atlantic Monthly Press

De Geus, Arie. (2002) *The Living Company.* Boston, MA: Harvard Business Review Press

Goerner, S., Dyck, R. and Lagerroos, D. (2008) *The New Science of Sustainability: Building a Foundation for Great Change.* Chapel Hill, NC: Triangle Center for Complex Systems, distributed by Gabriola Island, BC, Canada: New Society Publishers

Goerner, S., Lietaer, B., and Ulanowicz, R. (2009) Quantifying economic sustainability: Implications for free enterprise, theory, policy and practice. *Ecological Economics,* 69 (1), p76-81

Jacobs, J. (1984) *Cities and the Wealth of Nations.* New York: Random House

Salingaros, Nikos A. (2003) "Connecting the Fractal City," Keynote Speech, 5th Biennial of Towns and Town Planners in Europe (Barcelona, April 2003). Available on World Wide Web under *Fractal Cities*

Odum, H.T. (2007) Environment, Power, and Society for the Twenty-First Century: The Hierarchy of Energy. New York: Columbia University Press

Cobb, C., Halstead, T. & Rowe, J. (1995) If the GDP is up, why is America down? *Atlantic Monthly,* 276(4), October, p51-58

Ulanowicz R.E. (1986) *Growth and Development Ecosystems Phenomenology.* Berlin: Springer-Verlag

Ulanowicz, R.E., Bondavalli, C., and M.S. Egnotovich (1996) *Network Analysis of Trophic Dynamics in South Florida Ecosystems,* FY 96: *The Cypress Wetland Ecosystem.* Annual Report to the US Geological Service, University of Miami, Coral Gables, FL 33124

Ulanowicz, R.E., Goerner, S.J., Lietaer, B. & Gomez, R., 2009 Quantifying sustainability: Resilience, efficiency and the return of information theory. *Ecological Complexity,* 6(1), March, p27-36

Peters, E. E. (1994) *Fractal Market Analysis: Applying Chaos Theory to Investment and Economics.* New York: John Wiley & Sons

Notes

1 Though most economists are still trained in the centrality of equilibrium theory, work in such nonequilibrium, dissipative or far-from-equilibrium systems is long-standing and well developed. Furthermore, it is now clear that nonequilibrium is the norm with equilibrium being a rather rare exception. Consequently, instead of using bulky terms like 'nonequilibrium', we will simply talk about energy laws and energy network science (ENS)

2 This is a fictitious name for a real person

3 We call this the 'Walmart Effect' because policies that encourage big-box companies like Walmart to set up shop in one's home locale, have been shown to result in just such erosion of the surrounding small-scale business networks

WHITE GOODS/WASHING MACHINES
BUSINESS CASE STUDY

9

Chris Tuppen

Washing machines follow the linear model of 'take, make and dispose' with most users buying machines as cheaply as possible and throwing them away when they break down because they are too costly to fix. However, if we consider washing machines in a circular economy we discover that there are business models that offer more value to users and manufacturers.

This chapter explores such models as repair, refurbishment, the rental market, pay as you go and improving the longevity of machines. It also presents case studies of washing machine suppliers who are providing customers with robust machines that are made to be made again

Chris Tuppen has been involved in sustainability for more than 20 years. He runs Advancing Sustainability LLP and is an Honorary Professor at Keele University. He was previously BT's Chief Sustainability Officer.

chris.tuppen@advancingsustainability.com

Advancing Sustainability
www.advancingsustainability.com

In a country such as the UK, where white goods are cheap and labour is expensive, when a washing machine goes wrong it's a sad fact of life that it's often more cost effective to scrap it and buy a new one, than pay for it to be repaired.

Over the past 40 years the globalisation of supply chains, and especially the introduction of manufacturing in countries with low labour costs, has resulted in the average cost of washing machines dropping dramatically. According to Andy Trigg, who runs The White Goods help website[1], in 1973, a basic Hoover washing machine was £94.88; in 2012 prices[2] that's £987. By the 90s the price had risen to £400, but dropped in real terms to £625 at 2012 prices. And in 2012, it's possible to buy an equivalent basic washing machine for less than £200.

In addition, design changes and technology advances have improved both the efficiency of manufacture and operation. According to the Time to Change website[3], on average, today's washing machines use 34% less energy and 75% less water than a 1980 model.

All this seems too good to be true, and on the basis that there's no such thing as a free lunch, one senses it must come with a downside somewhere.

As the cost of a new machine has reduced, the business model has become more linear. Most modern machines have been designed to be manufactured at the lowest possible cost, not to be easy to repair, let alone disassembled for remanufacture. Certainly the reliability of machines has improved dramatically, and this has led to a reduced demand for washing machine repair engineers. But designing machines for lowest cost manufacture often makes the parts less accessible and thereby much more difficult to repair. For example, modern machines have fewer bolts holding them together, with components today often fixed using spot or sonic welding.

In addition, the use of cheap component parts means the average low cost machine will often last no more than 800 wash cycles before it goes wrong. The more expensive machines, designed for the domestic market, will run for several thousand cycles before they need repair or (more likely) replacement. Typical mid-range machines would normally be expected to run for around 2,000 to 3,000 cycles before needing repair, whereas high-end machines can last in excess of 8,000 cycles.

According to government statistics, 96% of UK homes have a washing machine[4] and in the average UK home it will be used about 270 times per year, implying the average domestic washing machine has a life of around 10 years. However, families with a number of children may do up to two to three washes per day, and, if they buy one of the low cost machines, they can't expect it to last much more than a year.

The Market Transformation Programme (MTP) says the average life of a washing machine is a rather precise 12.09 years[5]. However, using more recent figures from a major UK retailer who provided a UK sales volume of 2.5 million washing machines per annum, a derived average life can be calculated of 9.8 years.

The Time to Change website, funded by the Association of Manufacturers of Domestic Appliances, is there to encourage consumers to scrap old machines in favour of more efficient modern ones. However, from an environmental point of view, the operational use of energy is only part of the story. If a consumer is going to replace their machine on environmental grounds then they should take the whole lifecycle into account – from raw material extraction right through to end of life treatment – and not just the operational phase.

Using data from suitable lifecycle assessments (LCAs) it's possible to calculate the 'optimum' obsolescence point. That is the point in time at which it becomes better to replace a machine than maintain it.

Taking data from a comprehensive LCA[6] for the energy used at different stages of a typical washing machine's life cycle, and combining it with an estimated energy improvement per annum[7], an optimum obsolescence graph can be created.

This graph[8] shows the total lifecycle energy used per machine, per annum for different replacement periods (i.e., product life). The optimum obsolescence point is the point at which, over the life of the machine, the energy improvements of a new machine in the use phase become greater than the energy required to replace the old washing machine with a new one. This occurs when the graph reaches its minimum point which, in this case, is about 10 years. This means that scrapping a machine before 10 years is wasteful of energy, and the steep fall in the early years of life means scrapping much before five years is hugely wasteful.

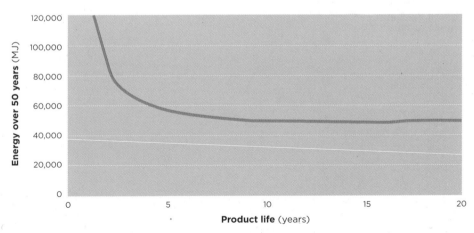

Figure 1 **The optimum obsolescence curve for a typical washing machine**

The UK Waste & Resources Action Programme (WRAP) has taken a somewhat different approach to assessing optimum obsolescence[9]. Using full environmental life cycle analysis data, and not just energy as in the example above, they compared immediate replacement of A and C energy rated, end of life machines, with post refurbished replacements using either A, A+ or A++ rated machines. In making their calculations they assumed the MTP average life of a washing machine of 12.09 years, running 274 wash loads per year. The following tables in figure 2 show the global warming potential impact results:

Global warning potential impact values (in Kg CO_2 eq) for the replacement versus refurbishment study scenarios for an 'A' rated household washing machine.

Replaced by	'A' rated machine replaced immediately	'A' rated machine refurbished, used for a further 3 years, then replaced	'A' rated machine refurbished, used for a further 6 years, then replaced	'A' rated machine refurbished, used for a further 9 years, then replaced
A++	1940	2030	2090	2150
A+	2290	2290	2260	2240
A	2420	2390	2330	2270

Global warning potential impact values (in Kg CO_2 eq) for the replacement versus refurbishment study scenarios for a 'C' rated household washing machine.

Replaced by	'C' rated machine replaced immediately	'C' rated machine refurbished, used for a further 3 years, then replaced	'C' rated machine refurbished, used for a further 6 years, then replaced	'C' rated machine refurbished, used for a further 9 years, then replaced
A++	1940	2060	2160	2250
A+	2290	2320	2330	2340
A	2420	2420	2400	2370

Notes
Colours in the table denote categories for percentage difference in impact values from the best performing scenario where:

0-10% difference from best performing scenario

10-20% difference from best performing scenario

20-30% difference from best performing scenario

Machines are either directly replaced immediately, or refurbished and then used for a further x years, then are subsequently replaced by either A++, or A rated machines for the remaining period.

Values in the tables are expressed in Kg CO_2 equiv the 12.09 year period (274 washes per year)

Figure 2 **WRAP global warming potential impacts for various replacement/refurbishment scenarios**

According to the WRAP analysis, in all cases it is undoubtedly better to replace either the A or C machine, with a new A++ machine than refurbish the original. For the other scenarios the case for refurbishment was at best marginal. In addition to the impacts of global warming potential, similar results were also obtained for resource depletion, acidification, photochemical oxidation, solid waste generation and water.

To a first approximation, the WRAP work is consistent with the 12-year life point in the optimum obsolescence graph shown in Figure 1. The conclusion that immediate replacement of either an A or C machine with an A++ machine is the best option is also consistent with the fact[10] that this represents the same as (in the case of an A machine), or faster (for a C machine), per annum efficiency gain than the 2.5% used in the optimum obsolescence calculation of Figure 1.

The WRAP finding may be counter intuitive to the circular economy preference for reuse and remanufacture. However, it's important to acknowledge it was based on a fixed life of 12.09 years and does not take into account the fact that many machines will fail before then – especially at the cheaper end of the market. For these machines, although a life extension is likely to be environmentally beneficial, the problem is it is unlikely to be cost effective.

Materials flows

In order fully to understand the issues surrounding the circular economy and washing machines it's important at this stage to look inside the machine, review the key components and the materials they are made from. Ignoring flashy bells and whistles on some devices, all washing machines essentially reduce to a few major components:

1. A painted steel case.
2. A transparent loading door.
3. Electrically controlled water entry valves.
4. A drive motor – usually connected to the drum by a belt but occasionally direct drive.
5. The washing drum – steel for the inner drum and plastic for the outer.
6. An electronic programmer.
7. A large concrete stabiliser block to stop it walking across the floor when it spins.
8. Miscellaneous hoses, plastic components, mounts and cables.

Based on the same Öko-Institut LCA as used for the optimum obsolescence graph, the distribution of materials by weight is shown in Figure 3. It is dominated by the plastic, steel and concrete. Whilst smaller in weight terms, there are also important levels of higher value copper from the electrical and plumbing components.

In the EU, Washing machines are covered by the Waste Electric and Electronic Equipment Directive and come under the large household appliances (LHA) category. According to the UK Environment Agency nearly 500,000 tonnes of LHA was placed on the UK market in 2010. In the same year just over 140,000 tonnes of LHA was recovered for recycling through official channels. This would imply a fairly low recycling rate of around 30%. However, the recycling industry believes that very little LHA goes to landfill which suggests a high recovery rate through unofficial, and therefore unrecorded, channels.

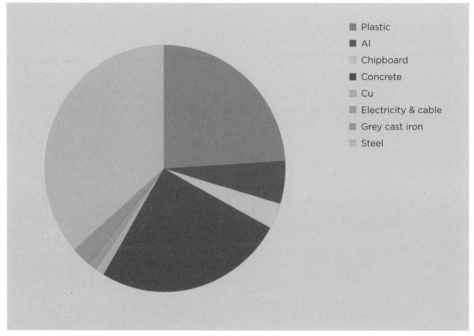

Figure 3 **Typical material distribution for a washing machine by weight**

There are also no official figures for levels of reuse but the recycling industry suggests this is very low, at no more than about 2% of the end of life machines that have actually entered the waste stream – that is excluding new machines damaged in transit, etc.

Based on the data presented above it is possible to calculate an approximate annual flow of materials used in UK washing machines, Figure 4. The most significant component, by weight, of the landfilled materials is the concrete stabilisation block. Figure 4 also shows the amount of electricity and water used by washing machines each year in the UK. These figures are telling, with 5 million tonnes of CO_2 representing just over 1% of all UK CO_2 emissions.

Washing machines in a circular economy
There is a range of actions that could be taken to improve the circularity of washing machines; some immediate and easy, others requiring a more fundamental change to the entire business model.

Repairing machines
Once upon a time washing machines were notoriously unreliable and, relative to today's machines, substantially more expensive. This meant that repairs were both inevitable and cost effective. Today, spare parts have become increasingly more expensive compared to the initial cost of a machine and in some cases it's no longer possible to purchase individual parts, only the entire sub-assembly. For example, some washing machines now have completely sealed outer drums that can't be stripped

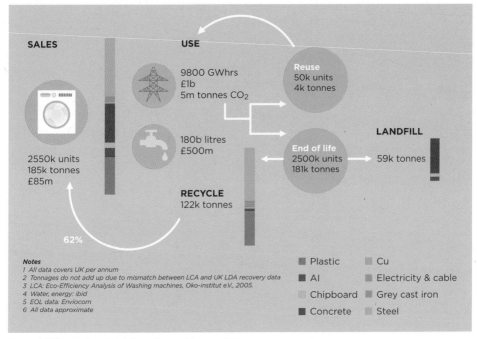

Figure 4 **UK annual material flows for washing machines**

down. Therefore, if a small but unretrievable obstruction, such as a coin, gets trapped in between the inner drum and outer drum then the entire drum will need to be replaced. Similarly, if the drum bearings fail and one can only buy a complete outer drum along with the inner drum, all seals and bearings pre-assembled, at over £200 plus £100 fitting for a machine that only cost £350 to buy in the first place, then there is only one economic outcome – off to the scrap heap.

The ISE case study (featured in this chapter) describes one of the few washing machine suppliers that actively encourages repair.

Reincarnating machines
One of the simplest changes to existing business behaviour is to recover machines from the waste stream and refurbish them. This can easily be done today and those who have tried it have found it to be profitable. However, most modern machines have not been designed with refurbishment in mind, which makes the process far more complex than it really needs to be. For example, while, in the past, machine components were screwed together, today there's a trend to use sonic welds or glue. This makes them much more difficult to disassemble and repair. For example, environCom (see case study featured in this chapter) is finding the front facia of some machines are now spot welded on when, previously, four simple screws had been used. This makes it far more difficult to remove the drum, as it now has to be taken out through the bottom of the machine – impossible for the average repair engineer to do in the domestic setting.

Even more worrying is the emergence of ultrasonically welded plastic outer drums. This makes it impossible to reach the drum bearings and will make refurbishment uneconomic in many cases. More standardisation of components would also help. For example, environCom finds the concrete stabilisation block to be different for almost every model.

Factors that facilitate a refurbishment model are:
1. A usage meter that counts the number of washing cycles.
2. In-built electronic diagnosis tools that provide a fault code.
3. Ease of disassembly and reassembly.
4. Ability to repair the sub-assemblies.
5. Easy access to the main wearing parts such as hoses, bearings and motor brushes.
6. Full, open access to repair manuals.
7. Good availability of low cost spare parts.
8. Standardisation of common parts.

In its report *Towards the Circular Economy*, The Ellen MacArthur Foundation modelled the economic case for the enhanced refurbishment of premium, long life washing machines across Europe. The transition scenario referenced in Figure 5 refers to a relatively conservative approach that assumes improvements in product design and reverse supply chain skills. This analysis calculated a typical profit of USD 93 for refurbishment of a USD 900 machine under today's trading conditions, increasing to USD 275 in the transition scenario. In both cases, refurbishment is more profitable than simple material recovery for recycling.

Remanufacturing machines is also an option, the difference between refurbishment and remanufacture being that the former creates a secondhand machine, often repaired with some previously used parts, and sold with a limited warranty. A remanufactured machine on the other hand is sold as if it were a new machine with a full manufacture's guarantee. This rarely, if ever, happens with washing machines.

Improving longevity
Washing machines that are well built and designed for a long life are inevitably going to cost more to buy. But being well built doesn't mean a machine will never break down and so such machines are only cost effective if the spare parts and cost of repair are economic. Unfortunately, this is not always the case and the problem can be exacerbated if competition is limited in the repair marketplace and consumers are restricted to only using the manufacturer's own service engineers.

Alternative business models
i) Spending more in the first place
If consumers were prepared to spend more up front for a washing machine then more, higher quality, longer lasting machines would be produced. However, many households, and especially cash poor ones find a lower upfront cost to be a hugely attractive proposition, especially if they need to borrow to purchase. That could be a very large number of households. According to Credit Action (now The Money Charity[11]), the Bank of England's 2010 survey of the financial position of British households found that unsecured debt was held by 52% of all households

USD per product[1], status quo and transition scenario	Refurbish		Recycle	
	Status quo	Transition	Status quo	Transition
Recoverable value	**560**	**560**	**38**	**38**
Treatment costs				
Collection and transport	12	12	12	12
Activity specific process (refurbishment or recycling)	80	80	14	14
Other[2]	80	80	0	0
Material costs	**297**	**161**	**0**	**0**
Profit	**93**	**228**	**12**	**12**
Net material cost savings	**140**	**275**	**38**	**38**
Improvements in product design and reverse cycle skills	40% decrease in material cost for refurbishment through pooled (OEM centralised) circular activities, as spare parts would not be subject to high trade margins currently observed			

1 Premium washing machine selling above USD 900 before VAT with average lifetime of 10,000 washing cycles
2 Other includes SG&A and other operating expenses

Source: Adrian Chapman et al., Remanufacturing in the U.K. – A snapshot of the U.K. remanufacturing industry; Centre for Remanufacturing & Reuse report, August 2010; Erik Sundin, Product and process design for successful remanufacturing, Linköping Studies in Science and Technology, Dissertation No. 906, 2004; Ina Rüdenauer and Carl-Otto Gensch, Eco-Efficiency Analysis of Washing Machines , Öko-Institut working paper, June 2008; Ellen MacArthur Foundation circular economy team

Figure 5 **The profitability of refurbishing high-end machines**

surveyed. In addition, Credit Action states that 38% of people say they struggle financially to reach payday, according to a quarterly survey by R3. This equates to 18 million individuals across the UK.

Even for cash rich households, lower upfront costs are always an attractive proposition, especially when the returns on investment are uncertain for the higher price machines. Such consumer behaviour has been extensively studied for domestic investment in energy efficiency measures[12], where individuals appear to have high effective discount rates of around 20% in making trade-offs between capital costs and expected operating costs. Purchasing a more expensive washing machine on the unguaranteed expectation of a longer life may well reflect similar behaviour.

ii) Rental
The obvious alternative to outright purchase is, of course, a rental model and whilst there are not many providers in the rental market it is quite possible to rent a washing machine in the UK. An internet based analysis of such offers from three providers offers an interesting insight to this market. For a selection of five low- to mid-range washing machines and washer driers, the rental cost over a two-year period was, on average, 65% more than an outright purchase price, including an extended warranty. An outright purchase can also be compared to the cost of taking out a personal loan to buy the same machine. At an APR of 20%, this route results in a total outlay of 122% of the initial purchase price. Rental deals also require a minimum rental period, typically in the range 17 to 24 months. Not only is the rental approach significantly more expensive,

but at the end of the two years the asset remains the property of the rental company. A further alternative is the rent-to-own model. In this case a weekly rent is paid and at the end of the rental period the customer owns term the asset. The UK charity Barnardo's examined this market place in their report *A Vicious Cycle – the heavy burden of credit on low income families*[13]. Barnardo's review of this approach found not only very high APRs, but also inflated initial costs which added further to the costs.

The *Towards a Circular Economy* report includes an economic modelling of a comparison between ownership of a low-end, short life machine and rental of a high-end, long life machine. This modelling finds it to be beneficial for both consumer and supplier to switch to a rental model.

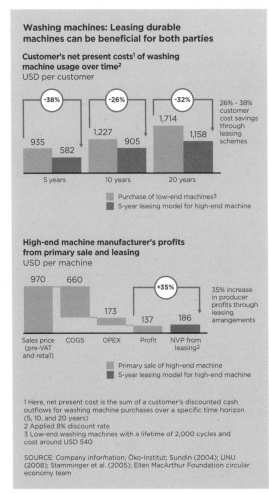

1 Here, net present cost is the sum of a customer's discounted cash outflows for washing machine purchases over a specific time horizon (5, 10, and 20 years)
2 Applied 8% discount rate
3 Low-end washing machines with a lifetime of 2,000 cycles and cost around USD 540

SOURCE: Company information; Öko-Institut; Sundin (2004); UNU (2008); Stamminger et al. (2005); Ellen MacArthur Foundation circular economy team

Figure 6 **An economic analysis of the rental model**

At first sight, the results of this theoretical model appear contradictory to the offers available to UK consumers today. However, the rental model does in fact look very attractive if it can be based on:

• machines designed to last for 15 to 20 years (more than 8,000 cycles);
• high reliability to minimise servicing costs; and
• long-term rental agreements with relatively low effective APRs.

For example, consider an ISE W288eco machine that is designed to last for more than 8,000 cycles, has a retail price of £999 and comes complete with a 10-year parts and labour warranty. If such a machine could be rented over 15 years with an equivalent APR of 11% and with a five-year extension on its warranty, then the calculated monthly rental would be considerably less than any of the currently available rental schemes for mid-range models. It is also highly comparable, in cost terms, to the outright purchase of a typical mid-range machine using a typical five-year 20% APR loan. Even for a cash rich consumer that would normally be tempted to go for the upfront capital cost of outright purchase, the advantage of such a rental approach is that it provides access to a higher quality machine than would otherwise have been purchased, without the risk of any expensive repair costs.

iii) Shared ownership

The third main candidate for alternative business models is a shared ownership approach. Of course, this is what happens in the case of a laundry service or use of a laundrette. Whilst the former saves on the time spent doing the washing, and often the ironing, the cost will be prohibitive for most people. On the other hand, a laundrette is going to be much less convenient.

Future Foundation finds that whilst European consumers are increasingly receptive to consider shared ownership models, this tends to be for items that are functional, infrequently used and have a high capital cost, such as a car for city dwellers. Washing machines are likely to be regarded more in line with the TV than the car in Figure 7.

iv) Pay as you go

The expected wide-spread adoption of smart electricity utility meters opens up the possibility of a pay-per-wash business approach. In this instance, the manufacturer would install a high-quality washing machine at low or zero upfront cost to the householder. The machine would then communicate back to the manufacturer via the smart meter every time it was used and the customer sent a regular bill. The *Towards a Circular Economy* report describes how this model was tried around 10 years ago without great success. However, the mass roll out of smart meters and increasing adoption of 'connected' domestic appliances make it timely to reinvestigate this approach.

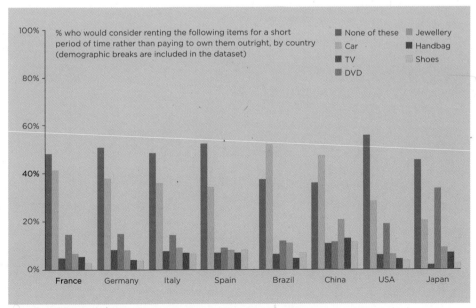

Figure 7 **European consumer views on temporary (shared) ownership** Future Foundation

Increasing circularity

Moving towards a more circular economy approach to our consumption of washing machines will require a reversal of the more linear tendencies of the last 20 years. This will require manufacturers, retailers and the financial sector to offer the consumer an attractive package, while maintaining the margins they already enjoy. The analysis in *Towards a Circular Economy,* and presented here, suggests it should be both possible and profitable. However, this is unlikely to happen entirely through market forces and may well need some level of government intervention to encourage this transition to take place.

A few interventions that would encourage movement in the right direction would include:

• Open source repair manuals. These should be made available over the internet for independent repairers to access.
• Machines to be fitted with easily accessible wash cycle counters.
• Guarantees to be stated in terms of years and numbers of wash cycles. For example, this machine is guaranteed for five years or 3,000 wash cycles, whichever occurs first. This is not dissimilar to some car warrantees.
• More cost effective finance deals to encourage the purchase of machines with longer lives.
• Feedback channels between the remanufacturers and the original manufacturers leading to better design for disassembly and repair.

The mass, energy and water flows arising from the use of washing machines in the UK as shown in Figure 4 are sufficiently large for the government to take a serious look at the situation and one would hope that this should, in and of itself, encourage the industry to be more proactive.

Notes

1 http://www.whitegoodshelp.co.uk/

2 http://www.thisismoney.co.uk/money/bills/article-1633409/Historic-inflation-calculator-value-money-changed-1900.html

3 http://www.t2c.org.uk/calculator/

4 http://www.statistics.gov.uk/cci/nugget.asp?id=868

5 BNW05: Assumptions underlying the energy projections for domestic washing machines, v3.1, DEFRA, 2008

6 Eco-Efficiency Analysis of Washing machines, Öko-Institut e.V. Geschäftsstelle Freiburg, 2005

7 In the calculation reported here an average energy improvement of 2.5%pa has been used for the use phase of the lifecycle. This lies in the middle of the range of values reported by references 3 and 6. A 1.5%pa improvement has been assumed for the manufacturing phase

8 Produced especially for this report, this graph is based on an improvement in energy consumption for the use phase of 2.5%pa which is consistent with references 3 and 4. It also assumes an improvement in energy consumption for the manufacturing phase of 1.5%pa

9 Environmental Life Cycle Assessment (LCA) Study of Replacement and Refurbishment options for household washing machines, WRAP, 2011

10 EU Regulation 1061/2010

11 http://themoneycharity.org.uk/media/february-2011.pdf

12 Policies for energy efficiency in the UK household sector, Oxera report for DEFRA, January 2006

13 A Vicious Cycle – the heavy burden of credit on low income families, Barnardo's, December 2011

Case study

ISE

ISE is a small washing machine supplier based in Kilmarnock, Scotland. The company's machines are designed to be robust, reliable and through a 'no parts mark up pledge' economic to repair when the guarantee period runs out. In fact the company's stated objective is to reduce the amount of washing machines sold each year. On the surface a very unusual approach for a business that depends on selling new products.

All ISE machines are made by Asko based in Vara, Sweden, in a factory that traditionally supplies commercial machines to the UK market. The machines are sold online and delivered and installed via a network of independent service engineers. Their standard model is designed to last at least 8,000 cycles and comes with a full 10-year parts and labour warranty. Components are made from engineered metal rather than moulded plastic and the highest grades of steel are used. ISE says this makes them four to six times more durable than good quality domestic machines, and more than 10 times more durable than 'value machines' sold by the major chains.

ISE encourages the longest possible life for its machines by selling spare parts at cost price and making technical information and diagnostics freely available to repairers. This makes ISE machines economic to repair and recondition after the guarantee period has run out, extending their life even further.

ISE also sells machines to large commercial customers, including a large hotel chain. The hotel chain buys new machines, uses them intensely and writes them down over a three year period. ISE then takes back the machines, remanufactures them for reuse and sells them at about one-third of the original cost. When ISE refurbishes one of these machines they will cosmetically clean it, change the bearings and motor brushes and make any other necessary repair, provided it is cost effective.

Case study

EnvironCom

EnvironCom is one of Europe's largest electronic and electrical equipment recycling facilities. The company has established a highly effective washing machine refurbishment stream as a more profitable alternative to the more usual approach of granulation and materials recovery.

When machines first arrive on site they go through a grading process. Older machines, those with small drum sizes and badly damaged machines will be rejected at this stage and will be sent directly to crushing. The remaining 35 to 40% of machines go to the refurbishment line where a second grading takes place. Here, a more detailed visual and mechanical examination takes place, with special attention on the bearings, filters, rubber seals, paintwork, etc.

After grading the machines into gold and silver categories a full fault diagnosis will then take place. The three most likely causes of faults are the drum bearings, the pump and the circuit board. Problems also arise due to faulty main motor brushes and bearings, wiring, heating elements and leaks. A machine with too many faults will be scrapped. Faulty components will be removed and replaced with repaired, or occasionally new, items. The faulty items are repaired on site and placed in stock.

Following repair, machines are given a brand new set of water feed hoses and then sent for a wet test involving two separate wash and spin cycles. They are then cleaned and finally sent for the mandatory portable appliance test (known as PAT).

EnvironCom refurbishment

IMPLEMENTING A CIRCULAR AND PERFORMANCE ECONOMY THROUGH BUSINESS MODEL INNOVATION

10

Christophe Sempels

Circular economy principles are quite simple to understand: closing the loop by reusing, repairing, remanufacturing, selling services rather than goods, either in a usage-based service format or an integrated solution delivering a particular result. However, implementing these principles in practice is not so easy, especially for incumbent companies, as it totally redefines the business model of the organisation. This chapter aims to introduce a method that could guide business leaders to innovate their business model and to engage in circular and performance economy that can lead to truly sustainable competitiveness.

Christophe Sempels is Professor of Sustainable Development and Strategy at Skema Business School (France). He specialises in business model innovation allowing companies to conciliate financial performance with environmental and social ones. He is particularly involved in the evolution toward circular and performance economy.

christophe.sempels@skema.edu

Skema Business School (France)
www.skema.edu/

Introduction

The various chapters in this book have largely demonstrated the unsustainability of a linear throughput economy at a macro economy level. When we focus on the companies' micro level, and when we question the vast majority of their business models, it is easy to understand that their situation is indeed environmentally and socially untenable, and that it begins to become economically untenable too. Many business models are volume based: the more a company wants to earn money the more it has to sell volume of products or services. Just think of an energy provider or a water management company that needs to sell more energy and more water to capture more financial value. How can they be truly sustainable when encouraging their customers to consume less would mean revenue destruction? The same is true for nearly every business.

In a context of limited resources – in other words when their price is under pressure – and when negative environmental and/or social externalities are systematically associated with endless growth, these volume based business models become untenable in all their aspects. This calls for a total redefinition of these business models so that decoupling can occur and both positive environmental and social externalities can be generated.

The goal of this chapter is to introduce business model innovation as an operational way to implement circular and performance economy in practice. We first introduce the concept of business model. We then describe the sustainable business model canvas, developed to support the transition to a circular economy. We finally address the main issues when switching to a circular economy based business model.

Business model and business model innovation

A business model is "the logic of the firm, the way it operates and how it creates value for its stakeholders" (Baden-Fuller, Demil, Lecocq and MacMillan, 2010). It defines "which activities a firm performs, how it performs them, and when it performs them as it uses its resources to create superior customer value and put itself in a position to appropriate the value" (Afuah, 2002). In general terms, it describes "the rationale of how an organisation creates, distributes and captures value" (Osterwalder and Pigneur, 2010).

Value creation comprises the definition of the value proposition and the consequent activities and resources necessary to its creation; value distribution comprises the definition of the "value chain required by the firm to create and distribute the offering and determine the complementary assets needed to support the firm's position in this chain" (Chesbrough and Rosenbloom, 2002); where the value capture (the profit equation) specifies "the revenue generation mechanism(s) for the firm, and estimate the cost structure and profit potential of producing the offering, given the value proposition and value chain structure chosen" (Chesbrough and Rosenbloom, 2002).

Switching from a linear economy model to a circular one may be viewed as a disruptive strategic innovation, first taking the form of a business model innovation. The processes of value creation, distribution and capture are profoundly impacted. Note that there are many barriers to business model innovation. Most incumbents in particular fail in this endeavour and disruptive innovation is normally brought by new entrants (Christensen, 1997). It may nevertheless be introduced by incumbents if their survival is under threat because an existing business model is unable to remain competitive.

To support the business model innovation, a prototyping tool may be useful. Inspired first by the business model canvas of Osterwalder and Pigneur (2010), a revised sustainable canvas has been formalised[1] to help business leaders to design innovative business models based on a circular and performance economy. More specifically, this sustainable canvas appears to be particularly relevant in a move toward one of these two configurations, even if it may be used in many other contexts[2]:

• Usage-based service: the provider no longer sells the product, but only its use (like leasing, renting, sharing and pooling). Far from being just a 'servicisation' switch, this model addresses the goal of decoupling the generation of wealth from the use of resources and energy. This could be reached either through revised manufacturing processes (closing the loop and promoting eco-efficiency; consider the well-known example of Xerox's leasing scheme with a close loop system for the copiers) and/or through the optimisation of use. This last option may be based on additional services that could reduce negative externalities. For example, SF Park[3] is a smartphone application that aims to find available parking places in San Francisco by collecting and distributing real-time information. Using the app, drivers can quickly find parking spaces, triggering a reduction in congestion and pollution emitted when circling the district to find a space.

Figure 1 **The SF Park system in San Francisco[4]**

• Result-based integrated solution: the provider sells an integrated solution (mix of products and services) that provides its beneficiaries with a final result that meets their needs. The solution is configured in a way that better balances the environmental and social externalities on the territory/ies where the company operates (reducing negative externalities and/or creating positive ones). Moreover, it relies much more heavily on intangible resources and tends to reduce the strategic importance of tangible resources in the related business model. This move generally redefines the scope of the business and induces new forms of collaboration among a system of actors implied in the design, the implementation and the use of the solution. For example, consider pesticides. Being stuck in a volume-based business model, the pesticides industry isn't about to reduce the production of this harmful product for the sake of the environment and the health of farmers and consumers. However, imagine a switch to a company that decided not to sell large volumes of pesticides, but instead offered an integrated solution for crop protection, guaranteeing a maximum acceptable loss rate on a specified crop. The pesticide gains to be reduced to its lowest rate as it becomes a cost to reach this rate. Moreover, every additional solution, such as the reintroduction of predators for parasites that could more naturally protect the crop, would become an economically desirable option. Environmental and social performance may now be conciliated with financial returns. But of course the changes required for such business model shifts are tremendous.

The sustainable business model canvas

Figure 2 introduces the sustainable business model canvas, structured around 10 business blocks. Before detailing all these blocks, readers should be aware of the systemic and interdependent characteristics of the canvas. It is systemic because it offers a full vision of the architecture of creation, distribution and capture of value. And it is interdependent as each block is related to the others, a modification to one box impacts them all.

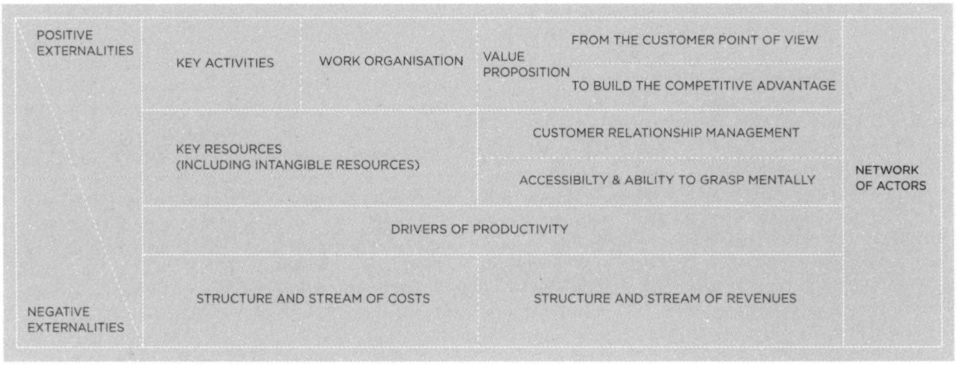

Figure 2 **The sustainable business model canvas**

This could be considered a prototyping tool, acting as a 'crash test' for an innovative business model, pointing out the weaknesses or the tension in the architecture of value creation, distribution and capture. It also becomes a powerful collaborative and communicating tool in order to get potential collaborators or investors on board. Let's now explore the canvas.

The value proposition

The value proposition is a core piece of the business model as it defines the solution that's proposed to the targeted customers. It is the reason why a customer chooses a particular company rather than another to solve a problem or satisfy a need. We have to keep in mind that an offer has no value per se. It only acquires value when it's able to convince a customer to buy and use it in a certain context. Before that, it only constitutes a proposition in the market. Therefore, the value proposition needs to focus on the customers it aims to serve and it should be formulated from the customer's viewpoint (attractiveness of the value proposition). Who do we plan to satisfy? What are their needs, their expectations? Which one of our customers' problems are we helping to solve? Are there any existing solutions on the market that could satisfy these needs? If so, what are our differentiating points and the added value of our proposition? It should properly balance the benefits obtained through the purchase or the use of the offer with the related monetary and non-monetary sacrifices. All these questions need to find convincing answers.

A value proposition should not only be attractive but also competitive, that means it should also strengthen the competitive advantage of the company.

Transition toward a circular/performance economy

The transition toward a circular and performance economy strongly impacts the nature and the form of the value proposition. The core part of the proposition is now a service rather than a good and the unit of invoice is sometimes difficult to define or to assess. Just imagine a water company such as Veolia or La Lyonnaise des Eaux that decides from now on not to base its income on volumes of water sold (expressed in a number of litres), but rather on service levels agreements (SLAs), generating positive environmental benefits. It therefore takes the form of an integrated solution beneficial for the environment. The SLAs should be defined to set up and measure the environmental gains. Are we talking about the reduction of leaks, the quality of the water, a reduction of X% of the energy consumed by the water treatment station? The contract becomes a core part of the value proposition as it should formalise the result to reach and the service level agreements that will assess the level of achievements. When selling an 'access' rather than the good itself, the primary competitor remains the traditional approach of buying the tangible good. Giving up one's car to think in terms of mobility solutions that are composed of different modes of transportation (public transportation, car or bike sharing systems, car rental for longer use) cannot be taken for granted for a vast majority of car owners. Designing the new value proposition to make it attractive for customers or to reduce its perceived risk is therefore not an easy task and often calls for innovative activities in areas such as R&D and marketing.

Network of actors

The network of actors (see Figure 2) refers both to the targeted customers that should be convinced to acquire and use the value proposition and the network of partners that are required to create the value proposition or make it available and accessible for their beneficiaries.

The goal here is to identify who are the customers, what are their needs or problems in order to properly design the corresponding value proposition. The ability for them to access the offer, both mentally (ability to be aware of the existence of the offer and ability to perceive its relevancy and added value) and physically should also be surveyed to ensure that the company is able to meet the demand in all its forms.

Regarding the partnerships, their types are numerous: strategic alliances between non competing organisations, buyer-supplier relationships, co-creation with some stakeholders, competition (cooperation between competitors on well-defined projects), joint ventures to develop new businesses ... are just some examples. And the motivation for partnering may be various also. A company may want to acquire specific resources or achieve collaboration on key activities; it may seek economies of scale or reduction of risk and uncertainty. Some partnerships may also be based only on financial support.

Transition toward a circular/performance economy

Moving to a circular and performance economy generally expands the network of actors and calls for a true system of actors. Consider the implementation of the Autolib in Paris. This project is of course particularly ambitious, but this car sharing system, based on electric vehicles, has required an important system of actors to design the solution, a "syndicat mixte" to coordinate a system composed of 46 municipalities, the operator company (Bolloré), a car manufacturer (Pininfarina/ Cecomp Italian group), financial partners (Region, Paris city and participating municipalities), city planners, geologists, the 'Architectes de France', mobility experts, water and gas companies, police prefecture and firemen... to define the stations locations, private and public parking operators and main public transport operators (SNCF, RATP) to integrate additional stations, an energy supplier and engineers to provide electricity for charging stations, an insurance company to create a new insurance policy for such a service.

If a subsystem of mobility such as Autolib requires such a big system of actors, just imagine the actors involved in organising an integrated mobility system that coordinates all the various mobility subsystems (Autolib, Velib, trains, tube, buses, taxis, car rentals, parking operators, highway tool services, telecom companies – to manage real time data required for such a coordination). The implementation of a single fare payment, which is the lowest level of integration, would require a strong partnership approach.

The impact is not only on the size of the system but on its composition. If the traditional sale of a product generally differentiates quite clearly, in this new situation above who are the customers (beneficiaries of the exchange) and who are the partners (part of the exchange but not the beneficiaries of it)? The transition

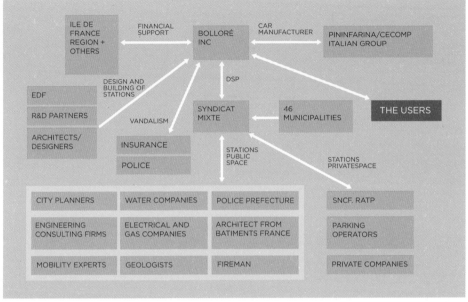

Figure 3 **The Autolib**
Source: Sempels and Hoffmann, 2011

toward a circular and performance economy sees a blurring of this distinction. By reconfiguring the externalities around an offer, an actor previously not the beneficiary of the result of the old product may now benefit from the solution. An agribusiness aiming to deliver an integrated solution to promote health through nutrition may now partner much more actively with a health-promoting institution that becomes both partner and beneficiary of the result of this service. Therefore, creating a win-win system becomes possible thanks to the redistribution of these externalities. Reducing negative externalities previously experienced by an actor, or inducing positive ones, favours an actor's support for the proposed solution.

Accessibility, ability to grasp mentally and customer relationship management
The traditional sale of tangible products calls for the implementation of distribution channels. These can be owned by the company or rely on partners, they can be direct (no intermediaries between the company and the customers such as web sales) or indirect. Distribution channels have different roles: raising awareness among customers about a company's value proposition; helping customers evaluate a company's value proposition; allowing customers access to the value proposition and to purchase or experience it (the delivery of the value proposition); providing post-purchase customer support. The configuration of channels may be the basis of a strong competitive advantage.

Beside the configuration of the distribution channels, and depending on their structure, a company has to define the kind of relationships it wants to promote with its customers. Ranging from dedicated personal assistance to self-service or automatised relationships (for example Amazon automatically suggests books to its readers based on personal tastes), the options are multiple. The relationship may be based on human interactions or not. It may be based only on technology. A mixed option is also possible, e.g. a bank that allows human interaction in its bank branch offices but also a self-banking platform on the internet. Co-creation with customers may be encouraged by dedicated processes. Supporting a true community of customers aiming to facilitate interactions between community members and allowing them exchanging ideas, knowledge and practices is another form of relationship.

Transition toward a circular/performance economy

The move toward a circular and performance economy needs to consider distribution channels and customer relationship management. First, the notion of distribution itself is generally associated with physical flows of matter and is strongly related to the industrial model.

In a 'servicisation' approach, it may be more relevant to talk about the way a service can be made available and accessible for the final users. The physical access to the service is certainly essential, but the ability to mentally grasp the service, its benefits and its result is also challenging. Zeithaml (1981) differentiates three kinds of qualities of goods and services. Search qualities are attributes which customers can determine prior to purchasing a product. The comfort of a sofa may be experienced before buying the sofa and is easily accessible. Experience qualities can only be discerned after purchase or during consumption. For example, the level of quality of a restaurant is perceived while the service is experienced. Finally, credence qualities are characteristics which the consumer may find impossible to evaluate even after purchase and consumption. The maintenance of a car belongs to such a category. For example, a car owner might take his or her car to the repair centre in the morning and get it back in the evening without being able to truly assess the work that has been achieved on the vehicle.

Tangible goods are high in search qualities while services are high in experience and/or credence qualities, generating difficulties in terms of evaluation and thus associated perceived risks. Switching to a performance economy model, either based on usage or results (the latter is more challenging), increases the level of experience and/or credence qualities and the related difficulties to evaluate the value proposition, its benefits or its result prior and sometimes even during or after the purchase. The question of 'mental ownership' is therefore crucial. The value proposition should indeed convey the benefits but the company should maximise the ability for customers to properly perceive them. Specific activities to support this mental ownership by the different actors are therefore needed. Moreover, the management of perceived risk associated with this 'fuzzy' and uneasy perception should be managed. Buying pesticides, for example, is quite an easy task. Signing a contract based on a promise of maximum acceptable loss rate on the crops is another story. Confidence and trust in the ability of the provider to reach the goals are absolutely essential and the company should provide signals of its ability to reach the promised result. From a customer relationship point of view, the relation replaces the transaction in a performance economy context. When buying a washing machine, the focus of the company is on the transaction, the maintenance of the machine being the responsibility of the user. However, when proposing a pay per wash machine, the company remains liable to the proper functioning of the machine. Every failure is a service interruption that should be solved rapidly. When delivering an integrated crop protection management service, the company provider should aim to co-create the service with the farmer so that the relation takes precedence over the transaction. Co-creation with actors is much more frequent in a circular and performance economy as the result depends quite often on the behaviours and the contribution of both service provider, beneficiaries and partners.

Key resources, key activities and work organisation

Implementing a business in practice calls for resources and activities that are strongly related. Developing a value proposition, making it physically available and mentally clear, managing the customers' relationship, delivering and monitoring the service, managing all the support business functions (such as finance, human resource management) need dedicated activities: R&D, manufacturing, IT development, marketing and sales activities, support activities, after-sales services. Activities refer thus to what a business has to do to run the company while work organisation answers the question 'how do we have to do what we have to do?'

All businesses are structured around activities but none have equal importance. Some are simply necessary while others are the cornerstone of the competitive advantage of the company. The latter should be carefully managed as they are highly strategic. The formalisation of the business model should identify these activities and their relative strategic importance.

Work organisation directly contributes to the competitiveness of a company. Two companies deploying the same kinds of activities (e.g. car manufacturers that have R&D, production and marketing) may differ substantially in their competitiveness depending on the way they organise the work. It encompasses the corporate culture, the organisational processes, the intangible investments, the human resource policy and the organisational structure.

Organising and implementing activities requires resources that could be structured around four categories. Physical resources refer to equipment, facilities, buildings, vehicles, machines, distribution networks, etc. Human resources are naturally one key resource of every company, as are financial resources. Finally, intangible resources refers to knowledge, expertise, trust, brand value and brand image, perceived quality, cooperation, quality of relationships, etc.

As with activities, all resources do not have the same strategic importance. The nature of the business, its positioning and its added value impact on the importance of resources. A consultancy company heavily depends on human resources and all the intellectual and intangible resources they own. The ability for a car manufacturer to be competitive depends of course on its R&D capabilities (and then on all the related intangible resources) but also on the productivity of the manufacturing chains and therefore on the quality and the performance of the equipment (such as robotics). It is fundamental for a company to identify and assess the relative strength of its key resources, key activities and organisational capabilities compared to competitors. A primary focus should be to properly manage them and to enhance their strengths over time.

Transition toward a circular/performance economy

The implementation of a circular/performance economy based business model impacts the key activities and the key resources. Here are some examples of such influences.

Closing the loop redefines the supply chain and the logistics flows. When Xerox implemented its closed loop system of copiers, it had to implement a reverse logistic flow as retaining the ownership of the machine meant they would get it back. Also, the recovery of the components of old machines to make them available for a new generation of machines required the company to redesign the machine by following an eco-design approach (thus calling for the related R&D activities). A machine easy to disassemble and to repair, a selection of components that last long, an increased robustness designed for more intensive and longer usage are examples of specifications for this redesign. Moreover, from a manufacturing point of view, a remanufacturing programme was implemented and industrialised. The impacts on the activities of the company were thus important, such as the impact on the organisation of work.

As previously discussed, marketing may become quite strategic for different reasons. First, these business models are quite new and people are not familiar with them. Markets should therefore be both created and educated, which may require some marketing efforts. Second, the perceived benefits or the ability to properly grasp the results are not always straightforward, calling once again for marketing. The added value of the performance economy approach should be demonstrated. The organisation of the co-creation and the management of the network of actors become an important activity that should not be minimised. The last point is important. Indeed, the need for additional activities (and the same holds for resources) means, generally, a need for additional partners. But because externalities are reconfigured, it may be easier to find those partners and to create with them win-win collaboration. Remember the systemic and interdependent character of this canvas.

Without being exhaustive, a result-based integrated solution relies heavily on a contract, as discussed in the value proposition section. The ability to monitor the service level agreements contractually defined also becomes a key activity, calling for transparent governance as this monitoring will determine the units of invoice and should therefore be verifiable by the customers and potentially by some partners.

The impact on resources is also important, the main one being the rising importance of intangible resources in such models. A circular/performance economy by nature relies more heavily on intangible resources and tends to reduce tangible ones. Selling a maximum acceptable loss rate on a crop, rather than pesticides, calls for additional expertise alongside chemistry and agronomy. The integrated solution will also require, for example, entomology expertise, biodynamic insights and traditional knowledge. Moreover, a co-creation with the farmer should be designed in a way that calls for trust, cooperation, transparency and listening capabilities. Developing a smart mobility system relies heavily on knowledge and real-time data to integrate and coordinate different modes of transportation. A broader range of expertise is generally needed as the scope of the business may expand, especially in the result-based integrated solution. The strategic importance of these intangible resources implies intangible investments with major strategic significance.

The drivers of productivity

Productivity refers to the amount of outputs per unit of inputs (labour, equipment and capital). It is closely related to the efficiency of an organisation and its ability to be competitive in its markets. Traditionally, the drivers of productivity are anchored in the industrial model: economies of scale, learning experience, work intensification and automation and ICT technology.

By switching from a product to a service logic, new drivers of productivity appear that could help rejuvenate the competitiveness of a company. Here is a non-exhaustive list of new drivers:

• The flexibility gains related to the working time arrangements, more flexible work contracts and the usage of nomad and flexible technology

• The adoption gains related to the learning effect induced by a long lasting relationship. Just imagine you had to change your doctor every six months. What a loss of time and efficiency as you would then need to explain your personal situation and condition from scratch at every change. A long lasting relationship is much more efficient as you know the doctor and he/she knows you as well.

• The complementary gains are closely related to the quality of a cooperation that could improve over time between partners. As already discussed, the transition toward performance economy calls most of the time for a larger network of actors, each one complementing the others to improve the efficiency of the whole system.

• The integration gains (mostly intangible) are related to the associated benefits of the integration of various uncoordinated products and services into a consistent and organised system. A global mobility system, for example, composed of coordinated and interconnected modes of transportation will be more efficient than the sum of uncoordinated sub-systems of transport.

The revenue model

The revenue model aims to formalise the process of value capture. The deployment of activities, the acquisition and management of resources, the structuring of the supply chain, the configuration of the channels to make the value proposition available for the system of actors, the management of partnerships and relationships, all these generate costs that should be covered by a revenue stream.

The two related business blocks of the sustainable business model canvas (Figure 2) are important and should identify:

• The structure and the stream of costs: the percentage of each element of the cost structure should be specified to understand the different financial masses. This block should also differentiate fixed costs from variable ones, ideally it would convert as many fixed costs as possible into variables ones.

• The structure and the stream of revenue: the specification of the unit of invoice is necessary. Note that there are various revenue models. The asset sales price seems obvious but it lacks relevance in a performance economy model. Usage fees, subscription fees, lending, renting or leasing fees and success fees are generally more relevant. In some case, licensing may make sense, or a brokerage fee. Finally, some models may rely on advertising to generate a part of their income. The pricing mechanisms may also be based on a fixed menu pricing or on a dynamic one, depending on the context.

Transition toward a circular/performance economy

The transition toward a circular and performance economy on the revenue model primarily impacts the construction of the income, the cash-flow streams and the capital requirements. Rather than selling a product, which is easy to implement in terms of value capture (asset price), the delivery of a usage-based service or a result-based integrated solution questions the unit of invoice. Michelin has designed a value proposition invoicing travelled miles. La Lyonnaise des Eaux in France has designed contracts where its income depends on its ability to reach targeted environmental goals, e.g. a reduction of a percentage of leaks in the network or a decrease in the energy consumption of the water treatment station. Koppert, providing systems of natural pollination and integrated pest management, invoices by hectares of fields protected. The right unit of invoice should be identified and should be easy to measure.

The transition from the sales of a tangible good to the provision of a service has also profound impact on the cash flow. Selling a product at a defined price means an instant recovery of the cost plus margin. Renting a copier, getting a pay per wash fee for a washing machine in use, mean negative cash flows over several months before recovering costs and earning money. The capital requirement is therefore higher at the beginning.

From a cost perspective, the impact of such a transition is also important. Decoupling being a core objective of the transition, the cost of energy and raw materials should decrease after initial investment to engage in the move. For example, Xerox estimates a USD 250 million annual saving on the remanufacturing processes of their copiers (see Sempels and Hoffmann, 2012).

Finally, the reconfiguration of the externalities usually generates the possibility for a company to monetise some benefits or share costs that were impossible to transform into value before. The agribusiness involved in the promotion of integrated health solutions through nutrition would benefit from the full support of health promotion institutions, sharing the cost of educating the customers and promoting its solution.

Finally.... positive and negative externalities

Externalities refer to situations when the effect of production or consumption of goods and services imposes costs or benefits on others which are not reflected in the prices charged for the goods and services being provided (OECD dictionary). Externalities may be positive or negative and may concern both environmental and social aspects.

• Smoke and toxic clouds, noise from a factory or a production process, the smell from an industrial process, the increased traffic on a given area, landslides and subsidence (e.g. related to mining activities), pollution of groundwater, the discharge of pollutants in the river penalising a downstream actor, flood induction (e.g. due to certain agricultural practices), depletion of an economic zone by relocation, destabilisation of a local community, ... these are examples of negative externalities.

• Clean air, a pleasant landscape, the absence of noise, bee pollination promoting better tree performance, restoration or protection of biodiversity (e.g. by protecting water catchment area), prevention of flood (e.g. thanks to some agricultural practices), carbon sequestration, protection against natural hazards (e.g. pastoralism reduces the risk of fire in the forest), conservation expertise, relocation and revitalisation of an economically underprivileged area, the creation of social capital, ... these are example of positive externalities.

These two last blocks of the sustainable business model canvas (see Figure 2) aim to specify the positive and the negatives externalities induced by the model. They are core in terms of sustainability as they will help to assess the environmental and the social performance of the business model alongside its traditional financial one.

Transition toward a circular/performance economy

A normative goal of transition toward a circular and performance economy is to reconfigure these externalities. The new model should therefore be more efficient than the goods-based business model in its ability to generate a positive net impact on environmental and/or social externalities. A first analysis of the externalities induced by the traditional sales of the product may be a good place from which to start building the new value proposition and to define the new system of actors. Moreover, the territories where the company operates may contribute to highlight externalities that would benefit from reconfiguration through the innovative business model.

Conclusion

The relevance of the sustainable business model to support the implementation of a circular or a performance economic model is strong. The canvas offers a means to prototype and structure the innovation process, and offers a systemic and interdependent vision of the firm. The robustness, the reality and the feasibility of this strategic evolution can be tested by constantly improving the construction of the business model through back and forth movements in the building of the different blocks. It points out the key challenges that require innovations. And, last but not least, it supports the collaboration and the ability to communicate with collaborators and customers, which is absolutely necessary if they are to embark on this fascinating journey.

References

Afuah, A. (2002) *Innovation Management: Strategies, Implementation, and Profits*, 2nd ed., New York: Oxford University Press

Baden-Fuller, C., Demil, B., Lecocq, X. and MacMillan, I. (2010) *Editorial, Long Range Planning*, 43 (2-3), p143-145

Chesbrough, H. and Rosenbloom, R. S. (2002) The role of the business model in capturing value from innovation: evidence from Xerox corporation's technology spin-off companies, *Industrial and Corporate Change*, 11(3), p529

Christensen, C. (1997) *The Innovator's Dilemma*, Harvard Business School Press, Cambridge

Osterwalder, A. and Pigneur, Y. (2010) *Business model generation*, John Wiley & Sons, Hoboken, New Jersey

Sempels C. and Hoffmann J. (2011) The role of value constellation innovation to develop sustainable service systems, *The 2011 Naples Forum on Service: Service-dominant Logic, Service Science and Network theory*, June 14-17, Capri, Italy

Sempels, C. and Hoffmann, J. (2012) *Les business models du futur : créer de la valeur dans un monde aux ressources limitées*, Editions Pearson, Paris. (the international version will be published in English at the end of 2013)

Zeithaml, V.A. (1981) How consumer evaluation processes differ between goods and services, In C.H. Lovelock (1984), *Services Marketing* (p39-47). New Jersey: Prentice-Hall, Englewoods Cliffs

Notes

1 This tool has been formalised by Christophe Sempels and Christian Du Tertre and largely used in a pilot experimentation organised by the Alliances CSR Network and the Centre des Jeunes Dirigeants (Centre for Young CEOs). This pilot project is aimed at supporting 22 CEOs of French companies to move to a performance economy

2 See Sempels and Hoffmann (2012) for a full description of these configurations

3 See http://sfpark.org/ for further information

4 Source of the image: http://sfpark.org/how-it-works/the-sensors/ and https://www.baycitizen.org/news/transportation/clog-streets-pay-premium/

REMANUFACTURING – A PROVEN BUSINESS MODEL FOR THE CIRCULAR ECONOMY

11

Peter Hopkinson and David Spicer

This chapter examines remanufacturing as one value creating business model. It provides real examples on the myriad aspects of this business model by exploring, in detail, Ricoh remanufacturing in the UK. Issues that are tackled include the term remanufacturing and how it is recognised and defined, the size and scale of the remanufacturing sector, the benefits for consumers and producers, opportunities and barriers and remanufacturing in the context of the circular economy.

Peter Hopkinson is Professor of Innovation and Environmental Strategy at Bradford University School of Management. Peter is now Director of the Centre for a Circular Economy and leads the university's Innovation, Enterprise and Circular Economy MBA and executive education courses developed in partnership with Ellen MacArthur Foundation.

p.g.hopkinson@bradford.ac.uk

David Spicer is Senior Lecturer in Organisational Change at Bradford University School of Management. His research is concerned with organisational learning, strategic adaptation and the management of change.
d.p.spicer@bradford.ac.uk

Bradford University School of Management
http://www.brad.ac.uk/management/programmes/mba/ distance-learning-mba/ circular-economy-mba/

Introduction

A circular economy is defined as an industrial system that is restorative or regenerative by design. It replaces the end of life concept with restoration, shifts business towards the use of renewable energy, eliminates the use of toxic chemicals, which impair re-use and aims for the elimination of waste through intelligent design of materials, products and systems and, within this, business models (Ellen MacArthur Foundation, 2012).

Figure 1 provides a diagrammatic representation of the circular economy as defined by the Ellen MacArthur Foundation. In this perspective there are a few ground rules and principles. The first is to design out waste and to re-think waste as food or nutrients for another process, product or system. To achieve this, products need to be designed and optimised for a cycle of disassembly and re-use, not necessarily in their original form or product cycle. These product and component cycles differentiate the circular economy from recycling or standard approaches to resource efficiency. To achieve this effectively requires a clear differentiation between technical (durable) and biological (decomposable) materials that can be returned safely to the biosphere in various cascading cycles. Technical materials, such as metals and polymers, are unsuitable to return to the biosphere but are capable of repeat use. These various cycles are shown in Figure 1 as a series of feedback loops.

The cycling of technical nutrients shifts the emphasis from consumption of products and to the notion of consumers as users. This is enabled through a shift in the business model of the relationship between producer and consumer to one based on product performance and access rather than ownership and consumption. Various familiar models for achieving this including rental, lease or collaborative consumption, or by providing financial incentives, when a product is sold, to encourage users to return them directly via third party systems.

These guiding principles and business models provide the opportunity for value creation that offer advantages to business, customers, the economy and management of stocks of natural capital compared to linear product and materials models (Ellen MacArthur Foundation/Mckinsey, 2012). Three of these are relevant to this chapter:

1) Minimising comparative material usage. The less a product has to be changed in reuse, remanufacture and refurbishment and the faster it returns to use, the higher the potential savings on the share of materials, energy, labour and capital embedded in the product and the attendant externalities.
2) Maximising the number of consecutive cycles (reuse, remanufacture, repair) and time in these cycles.
3) Using uncontaminated materials streams allows for greater efficiency in collection and redistribution, which maintains quality. This then extends product and material longevity and material productivity.

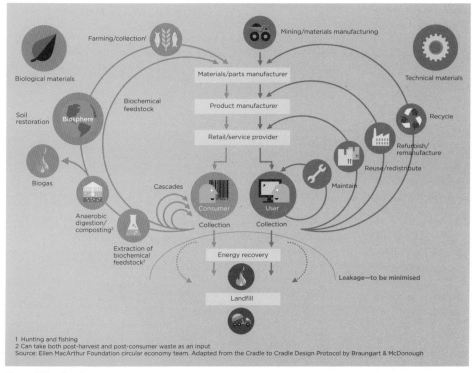

Figure 1 **The circular economy**

However, in order to achieve these benefits a shift is required against linear production systems and the design of reverse supply chains or closed loop supply chains, which is not straightforward. This then raises the questions of whether circularity can work in today's economic systems and if so where is it happening and why? If not then what needs to change?

In this chapter we examine one value creating business model – remanufacturing, for both proof of concept, and as a strategic business opportunity, within the circular economy perspective. The chapter is set out in four sections. Firstly, we define the term remanufacturing. Secondly, we describe the size and scale of the remanufacturing sector and the benefits to producers and consumers, including the materials, resource and energy benefits. Thirdly, we provide a case example, based on Ricoh remanufacturing UK, to illustrate materials and resource benefits, business drivers, opportunities and barriers. Finally, we highlight the prospects and critical issues for the acceleration of remanufacturing and the circular economy.

What is remanufacturing?

A key challenge in defining and assessing the scale of remanufacturing or repair and re-use activities is presented in the many and flexible ways in which those terms are used.

Parker (2007) defines remanufacture as the process of recovering an End of Life (EoL) product and carrying out required restoration to return it to at least Original Equipment Manufacturing (OEM) performance condition with a product warranty that at least equals that of a comparative product.

The United States International Trade Commission (USITC) defines remanufactured goods as entirely or partially comprised of parts that (i) have been obtained from the disassembly of used goods and (ii) have been processed, cleaned, inspected and tested to the extent necessary to ensure that they have been restored to original working conditions or better, and for which the remanufacturer has issued a warranty (USITC, 2012).

Re-use on the other hand, is defined by Parker (2007) as a generic term covering all operations where an EoL product is put back into service, essentially in the same form, with or without repair or remediation. EBay would represent an example of a business model where many products are exchanged for re-use. Re-use is different from recycling which involves processing the collected products into materials for new products. Repair is defined as the correction of specific faults in a product before it is put back into service.

More recently, the British Standards Institute has produced BS 8887-220 to provide an internationally recognised standard for terminology and kite-mark for re-manufactured products. BS 8887-220 specifies requirements for the process of remanufacture and lists the steps required to change a used product into an as-new product, with at least equivalent performance and warranty of a comparable new replacement product. Remanufacture is thus defined as returning a used product to at least its original performance with a warranty that is equivalent to or better than that of the newly manufactured product. From a customer viewpoint, the remanufactured product can be considered to be the same as the new product. For the manufacturer, manufacturing effort involves dismantling the product, the restoration and replacement of components and testing of the individual parts and whole product to ensure that it is within its original design specifications.

How big is the market?

The lack of a common definition has made it difficult in the past to assess the size and scale of the remanufacturing sector globally or nationally. A recent study by the United States International Trade Commission (USITC, 2012), however, provides a detailed, comprehensive and systematic study of remanufactured goods and clear evidence of the importance and scale of this sector. The US is the largest remanufacturer globally, worth approximately USD 43 Billion and providing 180,000 full-time US jobs, with SMEs accounting for 36% of employment (USITC, 2012).

Between 2009 and 2011 the value of this activity increased by 15%. US exports of remanufactured goods amounted to USD 11.7 billion in 2011. USITC (2012) reports that the automotive remanufacturing industry is valued at around USD 85-USD 100 billion and USD 40 billion in the US in 2009.

The major remanufacturing intensive industries are spread across a broad range of sectors, including aerospace, consumer products, electrical appliances, heavy duty and off road equipment. IT products, trains, machinery, medical devices, furniture, motor vehicle parts, restaurant equipment and retreaded tyres. Key features of these sectors are capital intensive goods, durable products and long product life cycles.

Remanufacturing is also well established in Europe with UK and Germany presenting the largest visible activity. An earlier study, Watson (2008), reports that remanufacturing is worth around £5 billion to the UK economy, primarily in the business-to-business field and represents savings of around 270,000 tonnes of raw materials per annum. Watson (2008) also reports that business-to-consumer relationships have been largely restricted to specific product categories (ink cartridges) and far less dynamic in embracing remanufacturing.

Although repair and refurbishment activities are common in many sectors across the world, remanufacturing as a distinct area of activity is relatively recent and trade in remanufactured goods is relatively small and often restricted to a local scale. Ironically, those markets experiencing the greatest demand for remanufactured items, such as Brazil, China and India, are also those that have the greatest restrictions or outright bans on remanufacturing (USITC, 2012). Widespread regulatory barriers in foreign markets affect trade in both remanufactured goods and cores (the used goods to be remanufactured). One key problem is the lack of a legally agreed or accepted definition of remanufacture, leading to such goods being classed for import as used goods – with attendant greater restrictions when compared with new goods, and remanufactured goods often being prohibited outright. Cores are also often banned from import, thereby reducing supply.

Various factors affect the ability of remanufactured goods to compete in home or foreign markets. In all cases the availability and relative prices of cores is critical. Other factors vary across products and sectors, including availability of skilled workers (e.g. aerospace), transportation costs, customers' preferences for new products (notably in short lifecycle consumer products), availability of low cost new products, energy costs or environmental regulations.

The potential benefits of remanufacturing are significant. Giuntini and Guadette (2003), for example, report that remanufactured products cost 40-65% less to produce and are typically 30-40% cheaper for the customer. Matsumoto and Umeda (2011) report that in specific cases, such as photocopiers, 93% (by weight) of a typical remanufactured machine is composed of reused parts whilst its price is 50-70% less than prices of new products and profit margins are higher.

Ricoh case study

To highlight and illustrate in greater detail the opportunities and barriers for remanufacturing in relation to a circular economy, the following case study, based on Ricoh, a well known global copier manufacturer, is presented. The focus of the case is the UK remanufacturing plant based in Telford.

The remanufacturing of copier machines is a well-known and reported example of remanufacturing, with Xerox, Fuji and Ricoh (accounting for about 90% of Japan's photocopier market) having long-standing remanufacturing businesses. Part of the success for remanufacturing in this product category derives from an established leasing business model, which arose at a time when individual machines were so expensive that they were generally rented rather than purchased. This rental, or leasing, and the return of machines, coupled with the need for frequent maintenance, meant that a reverse supply chain has been a key feature of the copier manufacturer business model from the outset.

Ricoh is a provider of managed document services, production printing, office solutions and IT services. It is a Fortune 500 company active in 180 countries.

Ricoh has been remanufacturing at its Telford site in the UK since the early 1990s. This site started as a production plant in 1985, producing copiers, printers, faxes and toner cartridges for the European market. At this time, import duties, introduced as anti-dumping measures, limited the viability and profitability of importing finished product to the UK and Europe and therefore the development of manufacturing (assembly) plants inside the European market was seen as a priority for Ricoh. Telford was chosen as a site for a UK plant in part because of the support provided by the local council, who saw the plant as beneficial for the local economy. Today, Ricoh employs around 900 people across the new and remanufacturing lines.

Initially, the site was successful and profitable in focusing on its core operations. However, by 1994, Ricoh was operating in Europe on a primarily leasing basis, and through growth (largely by acquisition) had reached a point where it recognised that its market was maturing and hence opportunities for further growth were limited. It was therefore clear to plant managers that commercial pressures, and the need to remain competitive and productive as a manufacturing site within Ricoh, meant that the Telford site needed to diversify its production activities. Remanufacturing was recognised as a potential opportunity in this regard.

Prior to the startup of remanufacturing at Telford, there had been little interest in or focus on remanufacturing in Ricoh. Ricoh did undertake local (in country) refurbishment, employing a model whereby assets such as copiers and printers were brought in and subject to a minimal level of reworking and then putting them back into local markets as secondhand/refurbished machines.

In the 1980s and 1990s, the typical production life cycle of a copier or printer would be between 18 months and three years. After this period products were replaced with new machinery. At that time, the primary driver for the company was to ensure a throughput of this (new) product in order to ensure that Telford and other factories remained busy and productive. Similarly, the drivers for the sales force were linked to this production cycle. They were therefore focused on and incentivised to encourage customers to upgrade to new machinery at the end of each lease contract. One consequence of this was that there were a lot of copiers and printers being returned at the end of lease periods, but which still had not reached anywhere near the end of their useful lifecycle.

Recognising that these machines represented an opportunity for Ricoh generally, and the Telford site in particular, Ricoh UK set up, at Telford, a centralised facility for the remanufacture of copiers and printers which could then be sold back into the market with the Ricoh brand on them. However, at this time, the company's approach was formally recognised internally as 'reconditioning' or 'refurbishment' rather than being seen or managed as remanufacturing, and it was managed separately from the core manufacturing business as a 'recycling division'. This perspective reflected the wider programme operating with Ricoh from the mid-1990s, the COMET circle (Figure 2), which promoted product design and materials recovery for re-use and recycling.

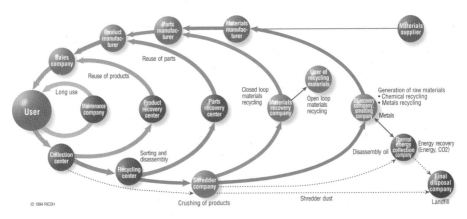

Figure 2 **The circular economy at work: Ricoh's Comet Circle™**

Initially, sales of 'remanufactured' machinery were made through the company's dealer network, rather than by leasing directly to customers. The advantages to Ricoh of this purchase (by the dealer) rather than a leasing business model, was that this product then ceased to be a company liability, with the ongoing risks associated with leasing (and the servicing and support of machinery) transferred to the dealers. In addition, it ensured further sales of toner and developer for these machines. From the dealer perspective, the advantages came in terms of the price offered and hence profit margins available on the remanufactured machinery.

Whilst the impetus and intention for the remanufacturing business at Telford was to take and remanufacture material from across Europe, the initial targets in terms of market size could be more than met through remanufacture of the product returned in the UK, hence there was no need for or demand to bring machines back to Telford from other European markets. As a result, this started off as, and remained, a largely UK based business.

This business model continued into the 2000s. However, early in this decade, Ricoh chose to refocus and develop its recycling infrastructure and the recycling division in the UK. This led to a much broader perspective and strategy asset recovery and reuse in Ricoh. It was at this time that remanufacturing was explicitly recognised as a business model and a formal infrastructure for the remanufacturing business, extending across the Ricoh supply chain, incorporating partners in the sales and operating companies, was set up. Remanufacturing also broadened in scope from the reconditioning of primary assets (copiers, printers and the like) to include consumables, such as cartridges.

A significant shift that supported the approach adopted by Ricoh from the early part of the 2000s was the increased recognition of remanufacturing as a viable business model. Customers were more willing to accept remanufactured product and margins on remanufactured copiers and printers being typically higher than for new machines, against prices that were typically 20-25% lower. The remanufacture process involves a complete stripping of the chassis (See Figure 3) and re-inspection and testing of each of the 600+ parts that make up a copier, replacing defective parts with new and re-building to the original specification, including:

• All panels sprayed
• All modifications fitted
• Firmware upgraded
• All data removed (total machine sanitisation)
• 100% factory QA test
• All counters re-set to zero
• Recycled products are backed by a complete OEM infrastructure
• Completely re-branded and sold as a unique model
• Full warranty issued with each unit

Figure 3 **Stripped chassis**

A comparison of the performance of the remanufactured model versus a comparator new model highlights the 'as good as' or improved performance required under British Standard BS 8887 and the much reduced CO_2 impact as a proxy for material intensity. Approximately 80% of the materials from the original machine are retained and re-used permitting an original machine to achieve a product life extension by a factor of two or three. (See Table 1.)

Table 1 **Product comparison: New vs. remanufactured copiers**

Differentiation measurements	New machine	Eco-line remanufactured machines
Performance quality	1% AQL	1% AQL
Mean copies between call out	19,000	27,000
Product quality	Original product specification	Original product specification
Safety standards (CE marking)	LV directive EMC directive	LV directive EMC directive
Appearance	Looks new	Looks new
Branding	New brand	Eco-line brand
Service cost	As original specification	As original specification
Data security	No data in machine	All data cleared from machine
CO_2 impact	40%	1%

Source: Ricoh, 2013

From Ricoh's perspective, the shift in market acceptance for remanufactured products meant that there was considerable value attached in the marketplace to their 'first life' product being factory remanufactured by Ricoh, as the original manufacturer, directly. British Standard BS 8887.2 has been important in Ricoh being able to market the remanufactured machinery as having been restored to its original manufacturing specification. Hence the product is 'as new'. This is significant because only Ricoh has access to their own original manufacturing specification and being able to restore to this represents a significant competitive advantage over reconditioned machines, which could potentially come from any supplier, working without the original specification. For example, in the UK public sector, standards and frameworks for buying equipment such as copiers, which act as the only channel to this market, prohibit the purchase of reconditioned equipment, but will allow remanufactured machinery, where this comes with the same warranty as a new piece of equipment.

At this time the business remained largely UK based and focused on the dealer network, but with some other small, direct business to, predominantly public sector, customers in the UK and other European markets which are closer geographically to the UK (France and Belgium). Supplying private sector businesses is hindered by the need for large volume/consistency of specifications which are difficult to guarantee with an unpredictable and variable supply of returned machines of different vintage and operating system. Further demand has been growing from buyers requiring environmentally sustainable, 'green' credentials.

Across Europe levels of uptake and sales of remanufactured units varied dramatically, and significant complexities for the growth of remanufacturing were created by the lack of homogeneity in the European market. Overall, therefore, the remanufacturing business for copiers and printers, both in the UK and Europe, was relatively small and remained distinct from mainstream operations. It was described by one manager in this period as a 'hobby business' within Ricoh. This is in contrast to other mainstream competitors, such as Xerox and Fujitsu, who had been undertaking remanufacturing for a much longer time. There has since been steady growth in remanufacturing of copiers and printers in the UK. This currently stands at approximately 5,500 units per year and about 6% of the market served by Ricoh. It therefore remains comparatively small in respect of the business overall.

Two linked factors impact on the levels of uptake of remanufactured copiers and printers: customer and sales force perceptions of this product. Whilst consumers have generally become more willing to consider remanufactured product this varies between sectors and countries. The UK is, for example, perhaps more developed in this regard, but it is the public sector in particular that has shown considerable interest in remanufactured product, whilst commercial customer uptake has been slower. The recent growth of remanufactured product has been aided by the downturn and pressures on public sector budgets, which have led to customers seeking lower cost solutions. Customers, again notably in the public sector, are attracted by the product's green credentials and as a consequence Ricoh has developed brands to differentiate remanufactured product based on its green credentials including 'Ecoline' and 'Greenline'.

In terms of sales force perceptions, Ricoh has faced issues in getting sales teams, focused on the sales of the core (new) product to push the remanufactured alternative. Whilst it has seen uptake with those sales people dealing with markets that value the 'green' credentials and lower cost solution offered (as indicated above), incentive structures for the sales force which aim to drive sales of new machinery and a reluctance to engage in understanding the different nature of the product have acted as a block on their willingness to push remanufactured machines.

Alongside copiers and printers, another significant development in remanufacturing in the 2000s was a move into remanufacturing of toner cartridges and other components for copiers and printers. The major advantages of remanufacturing components come from the efficiencies gained by service personnel swapping defective components for remanufactured items and bringing the faulty piece back which can then itself potentially be remanufactured.

The significant benefit from remanufacturing toner cartridges comes from the margin generated. This is two-thirds higher than that on a new one. Also, in terms of the business model, margins on new cartridge sales are shared with Ricoh corporate in Japan, but for remanufactured cartridges the margins sit entirely within the Ricoh UK profit and loss account. In addition, new and remanufactured cartridges are now sold side by side and are not differentiated to the consumer.

Remanufacturing guarantees the original specification and the only distinction is that in the case of remanufactured product, the packing indicates that the product may contain recycled parts. In all other respects they are identical, and therefore, from a customer perspective, it is essentially impossible to differentiate the two products, unless you see and understand the implications of the 'may contain recycled parts' statement. However, consumer perceptions of and willingness to return cartridges for remanufacture varied dramatically across markets. Return rates across Europe average around 20% but vary dramatically between those markets with strongly developed cultures and systems for return, such as Germany (35%) and those where this is less well developed, such as the UK (4%). In competition with this you have other suppliers refilling cartridges, which also have the effect of reducing the number of cartridges available in the remanufacturing supply chain.

The biggest challenge in developing the European cartridge remanufacturing business was, again, the complexity of the market. This necessitated dealing with 19 different operating companies in 19 different countries, each with their own supply chains buying individually from manufacturing in China and distributing product in their local markets in different ways. This complexity impacted on both copiers and printers and their consumables and, in response, the recycling division put considerable effort into internal marketing, selling the benefits of recycling and remanufacturing across the European Business Units.

Strategic overview
From a UK management perspective, the drivers for the development of the remanufacturing business in Telford in the 2000s were not just the strategic and commercial concerns facing Ricoh as a whole. There was also a concern to ensure the viability and long-term survival of this operation. Ricoh is managed corporately from Japan and decisions about where to manufacture are primarily cost and margin led and made globally, so manufacturing is likely to be located in the lowest cost environments, regardless of proximity to markets. 90% of Ricoh's market is based in Europe, yet the costs of shipping product from China (which is where Ricoh's manufacturing is predominantly located) to Europe are relatively low. This means that Ricoh UK and the Telford site might struggle to maintain competitiveness internally and at times in the 30 years of manufacturing at Telford its continued viability as a site has been questioned. The business and logistic models for remanufacturing are significantly different, however, and part of the drive, therefore, to build this business was linked to ensuring the continuation of operations in Telford. Ricoh's manufacturing in China is essentially a bulk business geared to large scale manufacturing operations (measured in terms of thousands of units per day). The plant and operations at Telford are much more small scale and managers recognised that it could not compete and maintain itself just through new machinery production. The different supply chain of remanufacturing, where product has to be

returned before reworking and then reshipped to new customers, and the costs of transportation and logistics for the small consignments this entails (especially inside the European market) mean that a closeness to the customer becomes a significant advantage. In addition, Telford has design and engineering capability focus around small run manufacturing and specialist products. These sit well with the capabilities required for remanufacturing.

More broadly, there has also been competition between the remanufacturing business and the core operations in a number of significant ways. Remanufactured copiers and printers have always been branded separately and targeted to particular niche (often public sector, as indicated above) markets. This is to ensure that it is clearly distinguishable from the core (new) product, and partly, given the importance of maintaining and growing market share to the business, to ensure that this market share is distinguished from (and not cannibalising) the core business's share of the market. It is only since 2011, that Infosource (the market research organisation that takes care of the office automation industry) has allowed remanufactured product to contribute to firms' overall market share figures. Prior to this, Ricoh and competitors had to be careful to ensure that they did not fulfil their market share requirements through remanufactured product.

In addition, Ricoh remains essentially a manufacturing driven organisation with significant capital and other resources invested in major manufacturing facilities in China. There is a tension between the maintenance of this core operation at the heart of the business and the growth of remanufacturing which has the potential to limit the market for and sales of new product. To date, there remains little direct interest in remanufacturing in the Chinese business, other than in respect of its potential impact on the core manufacturing operations.

Looking forward, remanufacturing, recycling and reuse are now explicitly recognised in Ricoh's corporate plans. This has moved from a matter of local interest and concern in the UK and Europe to a corporate agenda led by the CEO in Japan with explicit targets for sustainability and recycling set in the company's 2050 plan. This states, for example, that by 2020, 50% of Ricoh's materials will be recycled or reused. What part remanufacturing plays in this is yet to be decided.

Discussion and conclusions

At the start of this chapter we raised the question of whether circular business practices can operate at a profit and at scale in today's economic systems. We asked how this fulfils the key principles and requirements of a circular economy to cycle and cascade materials for repeat use to extract maximum return on resources employed (RORE).

The concept of remanufacturing represents a particularly interesting business model to achieve both profitability and product life extension and technical material cycling. In other words, remanufacturing has the potential to achieve significant savings on the share of materials, energy, labour and capital embedded in the product and the attendant externalities. The greater the number of cycles and length of time in each cycle then compounds the savings and benefits and profitability. There is therefore a great incentive to design products to achieve uncontaminated materials streams, develop business models to achieve greater efficiency in collection and redistribution and extend product and material longevity and productivity.

Remanufacturing is a USD 40 billion sector in the US, growing at 15% per annum and operating at profit in the business-to-business sector. It is especially prevalent in a wide range of engineering and ICT sectors involving products with high material value and long product lifecycles. The widespread use of lease, rent and hire business models in these sectors, i.e., the purchasing of product performance and access rather than ownership, is widely established and accepted.

The print and copier sector has a long-standing history of product and equipment leasing meaning a supply chain design for product reuse is central to the business model. The exact meaning of remanufacture versus other terms such as repair, refurbishment and re-use has not always been made clear, or used loosely, which has affected measurement of the size of the remanufacturing sector and also created some confusion amongst consumers who are sensitive to claims about secondhand or used products and their performance guarantee. Recent clarification and international agreements for remanufacturing terminology have been published by the British Standards Institution, which establishes remanufactured products as having at least the same performance and warranty as a new equivalent product.

RICOH is a Japanese global copier manufacturer with a portfolio of attendant products and services. Operating primarily in the B2B sector it has a long standing UK facility for the return and refurbishment of copiers progressively moving to a full remanufacturing operation in the mid 2002s, involving complete stripping and rebuild of a copier to achieve performance and warranty levels at least as good as new. This is now supported and verified through British Standard BS 88870-220.

Approximately 80% of the materials, by value and mass, are re-used in the remanufactured machine, producing significant resource savings and a wider profit margin than on new machines. A similar equation can be found for the remanufacture of printer cartridges.

The remanufacturing operation, although growing, is only around 6% of the UK plant output and until recently has been largely UK centric. In the past 12 months a new strategy to review the recycling and remanufacturing infrastructure across Europe, involving 19 countries each with their own culture, supply chain and market characteristics, has been introduced.

Building a remanufacturing culture within a global business that is still dominated by manufacture and throughput of new machines, located in the far east, presents a number of interesting and complex business challenges, including logistics, customer perception and acceptance, internal sales, field engineers and marketing incentives and KPIs and the strategies and key messages from the Japanese parent company. Resource spikes and volatility, however, have correlated with the growth of remanufacturing. Hence materials cycling and re-use are now becoming a key arm of Ricoh's long-term business strategy. From an almost accidental occurrence of events in 1994 Ricoh Telford, UK has led the way for remanufacturing and circular business practices, demonstrating that circular practices can operate at scale and profit in todays economic systems. Questions remain about how big and how fast remanufacturing will become in Ricoh and whether the success of remanufacturing in the B2B and high value products can be translated into B2C and lower value items. Our view is that that they can although judgements on this need to be made on a case by case basis.

Acknowledgement

We are grateful to Phil Hawkins from Ricoh UK who provided an interview as a background to this case study. The views and conclusions expressed in this paper are the sole responsibility of the authors.

References

British Standard 8887-220 (2010) *Design for manufacture, assembly, disassembly and end-of-life processing (MADE). The process of remanufacture. Specification.* British Standards Institution

Ellen MacArthur Foundation (2012) *Towards the circular economy – economic and business rationale for an accelerated transition.* Ellen MacArthur Foundation with analytics by McKinsey & Co

Giuntini, R. and Gaudette, K. (2003) *Remanufacturing: the next great opportunity for boosting US productivity.* Business Horizon 46(6), p41-48

Matsomoto, M. and Umeda, Y. (2011) *An analysis of remanufacturing practices in Japan. Journal of Remanufacturing.* 1:2 Springer Oon

Parker, D. (2007) *An introduction to remanufacturing. Oakdene Hollins.* Available at: http://www.remanufacturing.org. uk/pdf/reman_primer.pdf

Watson, M (2008) *Review of literature and research on public attitudes, perceptions and behaviour relating to remanufactured, repaired and reused products.* Oakdene Hollins. Available at, http://www.remanufacturing.org.uk/pdf/report_on_public_attitudes_perceptions_and_behaviour_relating_to_remanufactured_repaired_and_reused_products.pdf

United States International Trade Commission (2012) *Remanufactured Goods: An overview of the US and Global Industries, Markets and Trade. Investigation No 332-525.* USITC publication 4356. Washington DC

AFTERWORD

No business can escape the fact that global economic conditions, the status and future availability of affordable resources, energy supplies and a growing global population are creating an ever more complex business environment. The limitations and growing problems of the linear economic model, that has served us well for many decades, demands that business as usual is unlikely to be a winning strategy in the future. The framework of a circular economy, as set out in this reader, integrates many ideas from different sources in a way that offers a potential accelerated transition from an economy built on throughput to one based on feedback cycles and a systems perspective. Whilst many businesses have engaged with issues such as resource efficiency, corporate social reponsibility, ethics and waste minimisation for many years these are not generally seen as mainstream or central components of business school education. Trends in resources, energy, credit, growth/stagnation and externalities all point to the need for a re-think of business practices and strategies to shift business models in light of these constraints and challenges.

The circular economy provides a systems perspective and insights from living systems to examine alternatives and options that offer the potential for new ways of innovation. Within Bradford University School of Management and Kedge Business School we are already offering and running executive education, MBA, undergraduate and post graduate level courses and modules on the circular economy for our mainstream business students – our future business leaders. We have found that the circular economy framework provides a clear, practical and effective set of principles and thinking tools for challenging business as usual and for business re-design. Our view is that leading business schools are key to the transition to a new circular economic model, providing theoretical and practical grounding for future business leaders. The business and economic case for circular economic business models and pathways is beginning to emerge and therefore has a major role to play in business school curricula.

This new approach and way of thinking provides a different context for strategy, marketing, accounting, operational management, e-commerce, change management, finance and economics, HR and people management and indeed all the classic and mainstream themes and subject areas within a business school setting as well as essential linkages to other subject and disciplinary areas such as manufacturing, product design, materials science, engineering and built environment and life and natural sciences. Our view is that the circular economy provides a powerful framework for business thinking about the next industrial revolution – an economy and flows of products and services that are regenerative and restorative by intent. This book provides a thought provoking and at times radical re-think of business practices, economic modes of thought and the interaction between production-consumption cycles, and the role of materials, resources and energy within the economy. Above all else, however, the perspectives in the book offer the potential for a wave of business innovation and entrepreneurship at scale and across all areas of industry, business, and organisational activity. Businesses that are able to respond to, adapt and innovate around the circular economy will prosper.

Bernard Belletante, Dean,
Kedge Business School
(France)

Jon Reast, Dean,
Bradford University School
of Management (UK)